Chequered Conflict

Chequered Conflict

Maurice Hamilton

SIMON &
SCHUSTER

London · New York · Sydney · Toronto

A CBS COMPANY

First published in Great Britain in 2008 by Simon & Schuster UK Ltd
A CBS COMPANY

Copyright © 2008 by Maurice Hamilton

1 3 5 7 9 10 8 6 4 2

Simon & Schuster UK Ltd
Africa House
64–78 Kingsway
London WC2B 6AH

www.simonsays.co.uk

Simon & Schuster Australia
Sydney

A CIP catalogue record for this book is available
from the British Library.

ISBN: 978-1-84737-268-0

Typeset in Palatino by M Rules
Printed and bound in Great Britain by
Mackays of Chatham plc

CONTENTS

INTRODUCTION

Beneficiary to Benefactor

The McLaren headquarters has no equal in Formula One. The semicircular building, designed by Sir Norman Foster and built at an over-budget cost of £200 million, is an immaculate monument to Ron Dennis's craving for perfection. A desire by the former mechanic to get away from the dirty fingernail impression of his business resulted in this curving creation of glass, steel and chrome; the so-called McLaren Technical Centre is as far removed as it is possible to be from the traditional motor racing image of workbenches and girlie calendars. The shining structure on the outskirts of Woking in Surrey resembles the lobby of a minimalist hotel rather than the home of racing machinery generating noise and lubricated by oil and grease.

The trophy cabinet stretches as far as the eye can see. On Wednesday 6 December 2006, Dennis, in his role of chairman of the McLaren Group, clearly had hopes of increasing the silver-ware in 2007 when he addressed a lunch for the British media. Dennis was in a relaxed mood, as well he might have been knowing that he had signed the twice-world champion Fernando Alonso. However, the main purpose of the informal gathering around a large oval table in the executive dining room was to allow Dennis to voice his concerns and win the support of journalists when dealing with the arrival of his young protégé.

The start of the 2007 season may have been three months away but Dennis and his public relations team were already anxious about the exceptional media interest in Lewis Hamilton, a 21-year-old who had won championships in every junior category and was already showing promise during test sessions with the F1 team. The expectation was that Hamilton would score championship points by being among the first eight finishers in the opening races; perhaps a podium appearance might be possible at a later stage. A win? That could not be ruled out, but it was unlikely.

In any case, Dennis was more concerned about Hamilton being allowed to settle into a job that would involve commitments that went beyond simply driving the car. Each day at the racetrack would call for lengthy discussions with his engineers as well as tyre and engine technicians. Time would be taken up with sponsor commitments. Then there was the media, an element of the sport that Dennis, despite protestations to the contrary, had never truly understood. This lunch was to establish ground rules that, regardless of Dennis's best efforts, were always likely to be more honoured in the breach than the observance thanks to the groundswell of interest in a talented young driver who was British and of mixed race, a unique combination in F1. Dennis said:

> If the rules of engagement are fair and balanced, we will bend over backwards to be cooperative and fulfil the media's wishes for both Fernando and Lewis. But we have dug as deep as we can possibly dig within our own organization and we are really, really going to try hard to win races in next year's world championship. And that means that, when it comes to the drivers, we are going to try to create the best environment for them to succeed. Some of the young drivers in F1, because they are young, because the teams that they drive for want to get all the benefit of having them, end up doing a lot of media work and that can be very distracting from the job.

In other words, media access to Hamilton would be limited. It was obvious that Dennis, having had the foresight to spot Hamilton's potential at the age of thirteen, was utterly determined not to have progress at such a crucial stage ruined by a part of F1 that is, in his view, a necessary evil at best and an infuriating and potentially dangerous nuisance at worst. Dennis was not to know it, but he would be having more dealings with journalists than he had bargained for. A fixation with an overactive media would reach such a pitch that he would not be aware of treacherous developments within his own team.

Viewed from the air, the 157-acre McLaren site, with a lake and the high-tech building at its circular core, was designed to mirror the appearance of a pebble dropped into a pool of water as row upon row of trees radiate from the centre in leafy waves. Little did anyone realize that the ripple effect would eventually stretch to the home of McLaren's great rival in Italy. By the time the backwash from Ferrari had gathered serious momentum, the tidal effect would be motor racing's equivalent of a tsunami, one that would come close to tearing McLaren from its reputable roots.

Those present at that lunch on 6 December had no more idea of the impending disaster than they did of Hamilton's positive and colossal impact on F1 and its history books. The forthcoming battle looked encouraging, but no better than one of several high points in McLaren's illustrious past. The trophy cabinet on the floor beneath the executive dining room carried silverware from 1986. The most significant cup that year had been won by Alain Prost when, against the odds, the Frenchman had claimed the championship by winning the final race in Australia.

The parallels between that season and the one about to open would become increasingly significant as 2007 followed its dramatic and, at times, unbelievable course. Three contenders had gone to the championship wire on both occasions and, each time, the outsider would win as two of the drivers squabbled among themselves to the detriment of a title that ought to have belonged to their team. Nigel Mansell and Nelson Piquet of Williams-Honda had defeated each other in 1986, McLaren being the beneficiary. Twenty-one years later, McLaren would be the bene-factor as Kimi Räikkönen and Ferrari, 17 points behind with just two races to go, snatched the prize in a turnaround that was as well deserved as it was remarkable.

But 2007 would amount to more than the totting up of championship points at its conclusion. The point of interest would be the manner in which those points had been won. After several seasons when Michael Schumacher had rested his dominant right foot on F1's windpipe, 2007 would be refreshing because any one of four drivers – Alonso, Hamilton, Räikkönen and his team-mate Felipe Massa – was capable of winning each race, a situation that lasted right up to the final round in Brazil. It had been the same in 1986, all three drivers finding themselves, at some point during the Australian Grand Prix, in a position to win the title had the positions remained as they were. On each occasion, although decades apart, unexpected drama would affect the favourites, Mansell and Hamilton.

The only difference would be the sour taste pervading the loser's team and the sport in general at the end of 2007. In a season of intrigue and bitterness, two engineers – one from Ferrari and the other from McLaren – would elevate spying, pre-viously a low-key and amateurish practice, on to a high profile and dangerously invasive level. It would turn out to be ironic that, while Dennis was focusing on the media over lunch in his boardroom, a respected and highly paid member of his work-force in the office suite alongside was about to embark on a devious course of action that would have a more devastating effect on McLaren than the best efforts of the most wilful and wayward journalist.

Such a thing would have been unheard of in 1986, mainly because there was neither the technology to allow it nor the will to go that far. Much had changed in the period in between. Yet, as this at times incredible story unfolds, it will become clear that many aspects of a complex and compelling sport have remained exactly the same.

1

All Pals Together

From the moment Melbourne received the coveted slot as opening race of the season in 1996, The Stokehouse was certain to be popular. Overlooking St Kilda beach, the restaurant enjoyed consistently favourable reviews, making it a perfect dinner venue for F1 sponsors and their guests. In 2000, McLaren and Mercedes-Benz were the first to explore the possibility of using the restored 1920s building to welcome the F1 media to lunch at the start of a new season. It was an ideal location as the McLaren drivers could be interviewed on the balcony, the swaying palm trees and the pure blue of Port Phillip Bay beyond providing a perfect backdrop. Photographers would be few and far between, this mainly being an opportunity for motor sport writers to have casual conversations with team members between glasses of chilled Chardonnay. A typical menu would consist of shaved Parma prosciutto with roasted pear, followed by seared tuna and lightly smoked ocean trout. It was generally agreed among the journalistic cognoscenti that there had to be less pleasant ways to earn a living.

In 2007, the lunch shifted up a gear. Instead of a just a handful of photographers, there would be more than sixty responding to an attractive photo call set up by Vodafone. The telecommunications company, having shifted allegiance from Ferrari, wanted to make the most of a new role as title sponsor at Vodafone McLaren-Mercedes. More to the point, Vodafone were

Chequered Conflict

keen to capitalize on a significant change in the McLaren driver line-up. Not only would Fernando Alonso be moving to McLaren after four seasons with Renault, Lewis Hamilton would join the reigning world champion.

At this stage, Alonso was the main interest with Hamilton no more than an intriguing sidebar. The thrust of any story had to be the element of gamble. Having secured his second successive world title the previous year with seven victories, Alonso was joining a well-oiled operation that had somehow failed to win a single race in 2006. For their part McLaren, a team that needed to be fighting for the championship after coming off an appalling season, had taken on a 22-year-old novice who would be expected to finish on the podium on a regular basis. Hamilton had shown massive promise by winning championships as a junior driver. He was good-looking and confident. He was also black.

Ron Dennis, McLaren's CEO, insisted that Hamilton's race had nothing to do with the decision to sign him as a F1 driver. The choice was based on his talent. That would quickly prove to be the case. But, for the time being, Hamilton's role as the first full-time mixed-race driver with a top team had a news value that could not be denied. The ranks of photographers outside The Stokehouse were a testimony to that.

Lenses were directed towards the bay. The plan was to have Alonso and Hamilton delivered to the beach by boat, an unusual method of arrival but one that fitted both the local ambience and the sunshine of early March in Australia. After much discussion by two-way radio between intense PR people, the signal was given for the drivers to be dispatched from behind a water break on the left-hand side of the bay. As the inflatable dinghy with its powerful outboard motor swooshed into view, cameras began to click. This made a welcome alternative to the usual shots of drivers posing among the racing paraphernalia of a F1 paddock. It would also be one of the last occasions when the McLaren drivers would be completely comfortable in each other's company.

Alert to every opportunity, Vodafone had used the shoreline for the placement of banners to accompany two attractive girls waiting to welcome the guests as the dinghy nosed gently on to the beach. Dressed in white V-neck T-shirts and black shorts (supplied by Boss, a long-time McLaren clothing sponsor), Alonso and Hamilton came ashore and posed for photographs while, not by chance, examining their mobile phones as the Vodafone banners flapped alongside.

The drivers then walked up the beach to the decking of The Stokehouse where television crews were waiting. Security officials did their best to keep a public footpath, bordering the front of the building, open for bemused locals as they walked their dogs and took in the late morning air. This cosmopolitan mix was rounded off by a man on a microphone who clearly knew little about F1 judging by the way he confused Christian names and surnames as he referred to 'Lewis' and 'Alonso'. It was an unintentional gaff but one that presaged how Alonso would eventually feel about his standing within the team.

For the moment, Alonso had no reason to believe he would be anything other than the de facto number one driver. He knew that McLaren-Mercedes adopted a policy of equal treatment for both drivers but, as double-world champion, Alonso felt no need to push a demand for superior status. This would come as a matter of course as he raced alongside an apprentice to a trade that Alonso had mastered so convincingly.

It seemed just as logical to assume that F1 was entering an Alonso era following the retirement of Michael Schumacher at the end of 2006. Indeed, Alonso could not be blamed for believing that everything had turned out even better than he had imagined seventeen months before when he had agreed to leave Renault. That decision, instigated in Brazil at the final race of the 2005 season, had surprised the F1 world, not least Ron Dennis, the boss of McLaren:

We all thought the door [to Alonso] was firmly locked. The point where it became apparent that it was very clearly not locked was on the podium of the 2005 Brazilian Grand Prix. We had come first and second with our people [Juan Pablo Montoya and Kimi Räikkönen], they were hot and sticky and wiping themselves down around the back of the podium and drinking water. He [Alonso], having come third, was obviously very keen to get the whole thing over with even though he had just won the championship. It was one of those moments where we were alone for about a minute or so.

I might have said 'Congratulations on the world championship' or something. His response was along the lines of 'Well, the thing about you guys is that you make it so difficult because you keep developing your cars.'

I said, 'You could be part of it.' In addition, he just said, 'I'd like to be.' I was just stunned. I said, 'Are you serious?' and he said 'Yes.'

The two would meet in secrecy at the following race in Japan and the deal was completed almost immediately. It would turn out to be the smoothest aspect of a partnership that would quickly run into turbulent waters once the relationship began in earnest.

Alonso had been motivated by two things: Renault's future in F1 was uncertain at the time and Alonso felt he could deal with Montoya, assuming that Räikkönen left McLaren, as rumoured, for Ferrari in 2007. Montoya was very fast when the mood suited him but his unreliability was proven when he mysteriously damaged his shoulder, allegedly while playing tennis, and his inconsistency was evident in the occasional lacklustre performance. All of that became irrelevant when Montoya and McLaren suddenly parted company mid-season in 2006. The Colombian's place for the remaining eight races was taken by McLaren's test driver, Pedro de la Rosa, a capable performer who could be relied on to support the team and not cause problems while scoring championship points where he could.

In the background, meanwhile, rumours had gathered strength that McLaren would hire Hamilton for 2007. If Alonso had any doubts about beating Montoya, then he would have had even fewer about being challenged by Hamilton. After all, Alonso had seen off Michael Schumacher more than once. A greenhorn should not be a problem, regardless of his excellent track record thus far.

Dennis was intimate with Hamilton's racing history. The boy from Stevenage, north-west of London, had begun karting at the age of six, his efforts overseen by his father, Anthony. It was soon apparent that Lewis Hamilton had more to offer than the unique nature of his background, his grandfather, Davidson, having emigrated from Grenada in 1955. Lewis progressed through the various levels of karting, his success in the Cadet Championship requiring his presence as a 10-year-old at the *Autosport* Awards. This black-tie function in London's Grosvenor House is motor racing's equivalent of the Oscars and, as such, it is attended by the great and the good of the sport. McLaren had a particular interest thanks to supporting the McLaren/*Autosport* Young Driver scheme and Dennis was present in 1995. Having received his award on stage, Hamilton calmly walked to the McLaren table and told Dennis that he wanted to drive for his team one day.

Impressed by Hamilton's polite audacity, Dennis made a note to keep an eye on his progress. Three years later, a long-term contract was signed whereby McLaren, as part of their young driver programme, would pay for Hamilton's racing through Formula Three and GP2, the final stepping stones to F1. When Hamilton won championships at every stage and appeared to be worth a drive in F1, there was only one team with whom he could possibly make his debut. Montoya's hasty departure and Räikkönen's move to Ferrari for 2007 made a McLaren drive seem inevitable.

Chequered Conflict

Confounding confident speculation in the media, Dennis and Martin Whitmarsh, McLaren's chief operating officer, did not rush to commit themselves and it seemed that Hamilton might be consigned to a year of testing. Hamilton wanted none of that and was probably as relieved as anyone when his place as a full-time driver was confirmed on 24 November 2006. Now he was in Melbourne, race-ready but coming face to face for the first time with the inquisitive and sceptical members of the world's F1 media. Typically, Hamilton would deal with the occasion like a veteran.

Photographs and television interviews completed, Alonso and Hamilton moved up to the first floor where the journalists, waiting for lunch to be served, were seated around large circular tables filling the oblong room. The relaxed atmosphere set the tone as Mark Norris, a member of McLaren's marketing division, asked the anticipated questions of each driver in turn. The answers were equally predictable but at least it was copy for the journalists poised with notebooks and digital recorders.

'It's been a very, very long winter of testing,' said Hamilton when referring to the preparations, mainly in Spain, prior to the start of the season. He went on:

We've covered a lot of mileage and I was the second highest driver in terms of distance covered. I think Heikki Kovalainen was first, but I think I did something like 7600 kilometres. That's a lot to do in such a short space of time. But I'm extremely fit and feel very, very relaxed about that. I have done a lot of race distances and I really don't honestly feel I could be better prepared. I really don't think a year of testing would have prepared me any more. I have got another step to do, which is to learn about the race and the whole race weekend, but that is something I am used to.

Hamilton then dealt easily with the next question about driving alongside Alonso.

'Fernando is an extremely talented driver, as a two-time world champion, and I respect him and respect that position,' said Hamilton. 'We have to wait and see. I don't look at the team and say: "I am number two." We are both there to do a strong job for the team and we are both here to win. So we will see at the end of the day.'

Hamilton was making clear his intention to be joint number one driver, a point which would not have been lost on Alonso and one which he indirectly addressed while answering a question about how he was settling in at McLaren. Alonso said:

I think I'm in a better position than in the Renault team and I'm happy. It's a little bit easier, to be honest, to approach the races winning (the title) two times. I know how to approach races, how to prepare mentally and physically. I think a completely new challenge brings new motivation with a new team so we will try and repeat the success. At McLaren, I have found a great atmosphere, the people are really very focused on the target to come back with success and to regain the dominant position in F1, and I have to say thanks to the team for all the huge work they did in the winter. They have improved and developed the car a lot compared to last year.

When asked about his chances in the Australian Grand Prix, Alonso applied a caution fashioned by experience.

'You never know what is going to happen in the first race. The first race is quite different, quite surprising for everybody,' said Alonso. 'Winter testing is difficult to read. We have to be honest and realistic and see that the Ferrari has been really strong. We are very confident and we improved the car from the last test before Melbourne. So we should be very competitive as well.'

The subject moved on to Hamilton's first Grand Prix, Alonso

recalling his F1 debut at the same track with the humble Minardi team in 2001.

'I remember that was the first time I sat in the car. With the Minardi that year we had no winter testing because the car was not made,' said Alonso. 'So the first time I sat in the car was here in Melbourne and I remember being in the pit lane, I didn't know all the buttons and the switches on the steering wheel and it was a little bit of a mess.'

That highlighted an immediate difference between the two drivers. Whereas Alonso had done no testing, Hamilton was, as he had confirmed, better prepared in every way. Alonso may not have been familiar with the buttons on his steering wheel but Hamilton, having cradled the McLaren wheel with its eighteen buttons and dials on his lap while watching television during the winter, was completely intimate with this crucial piece of equipment. Small details such as that would make all the difference in a season that would be more intensely competitive than anyone present at The Stokehouse could have imagined.

In the meantime, Alonso was understandably self-assured. 'I think we have arrived here in Australia with a really competitive car and I think we can fight for victory,' he said. 'I feel really happy with the move and really confident for the championship.'

There is no doubt that he meant every word. That would change sooner than anyone expected. Alonso would be in the fight for the championship but it would be a torrid affair with three drivers neck-and-neck going into the final round and coming out of it covered by just one point. The last time F1 had produced such a climax had been in Australia twenty-one years before. The sport seemed less frenetic then, but the aching desire to win was exactly the same.

2
Lost for Words

Even if Rio de Janeiro had the equivalent of The Stokehouse, it would not have been used as a lunchtime venue for the well-being of F1's Fourth Estate in 1986. Such affairs were considered an unnecessary luxury in the days when the teams were just about coming to terms with the need for public relations officers, never mind spoon-feeding the media with carefully cultivated soundbites.

The Williams team, a championship contender that year, summed up the attitude of the day with their company name: 'Williams Grand Prix Engineering'. This stated very clearly that Frank Williams and his co-director, Patrick Head, were only interested in building racing cars and winning with them. It was not that they disliked the press – indeed, both men were engaging company – but there was the nagging feeling that journalists and their questions could be a tiresome diversion from the job in hand.

It was the same at McLaren. Dennis, who would come to see the media as an irritation, was five years into his tenure as joint owner of a F1 team that had been founded in 1966 by Bruce McLaren. When the New Zealander was killed while testing a McLaren sports car in 1970, his team spent a decade enjoying a couple of championships before descending into the role of also-ran. When Dennis took over, the positive effect of his efficient management technique quickly became apparent. McLaren drivers Niki Lauda and Alain Prost fought to the wire for the 1984 championship, Lauda winning by half a point, the smallest margin in the history of the sport. The pair continued to be consistently quick as the McLaren, with its TAG turbo engine, won six races in 1985. The Frenchman was an obvious favourite when the teams gathered in Rio de Janeiro for the start of the following season.

Ranged against Prost would be Ayrton Senna, the Brazilian beginning his second year with the sinister black and gold John Player Special Lotus. Chasing them both, a pair of Williams-Hondas driven by Nelson Piquet and Nigel Mansell. Significantly, in the light of what would happen at McLaren in 2007, both Williams drivers had equal status and it would cost them dear. Before they could go racing, however, the Williams team had to cope with some shocking news.

Returning to Nice airport from his team's final pre-season test session at the Paul Ricard circuit in the south of France, Frank Williams spun off the road in his hire car and landed upside down in a field, his neck taking the brunt of the impact. Williams, who was lucky to survive, would be a quadriplegic for the rest of his life. Despite this terrible setback, the team was professional and well organized enough to go racing without Williams for the first six months. Indeed, if anything, the near-fatal accident doubled the company's resolve to win this championship for their much-loved boss. Williams, who had raced Formula Three cars with more spectacle than success, did not feel bitter about the accident. 'I was going too fast and cocked it up,' was his succinct summary.

Twenty-one years later, as Williams sat in a wheelchair and watched over preparations by his beloved team for yet another season in F1, such an incident in a hire car had assumed anachronistic proportions. In 2007, team owners would rarely attend test sessions. These weekly nine-to-five routines had become such a humdrum part of F1 existence that the novelty value had long since passed. In the unlikely event of a team boss making the journey to Spain or wherever the test might be, he would travel by private jet at best; at worst by business class on a commercial airline with a chauffeur waiting at either end. The thought of getting behind the wheel of the 2007 equivalent of a Hertz Ford Sierra would be as unthinkable as meeting a member of the Royal Family on the London Underground.

In 1986, however, Williams was mindful of budgetary restrictions despite having won two of the drivers' championships in the previous five years. With a powerful Honda turbo engine in each of his cars, a third title seemed within reach as the grid formed at Rio's Jacarepaguá circuit on 23 March 1986.

Senna was on pole, with Mansell alongside. Never slow in coming forward, Mansell went on the attack as the leaders rushed down the back straight. The Williams drew alongside the Lotus on the approach to a fast left-hander. Senna squeezed Mansell just enough to have the Englishman back off slightly, but not enough to prevent the Williams from spinning into the crash barrier. The season was only a few minutes old and Mansell was its first retirement as he flung his steering wheel from the cockpit in disgust. Such a display of displeasure would shortly be banned since the absence of a steering wheel would present marshals with a considerable problem as they attempted to move an abandoned car to a safe place. Mansell stomped back to the pits and spoke with Ann Bradshaw, the Williams press officer.

'I'm just lost for words,' said Mansell, before going on to prove himself wrong. 'I was ahead of Senna and inside of him, yet he still pulled right across me. I could go on, but I'll probably say something I will later regret. I have lost count of the times Senna has now either tried or has run me off the road.' It was to be an appropriate start to a dramatic year for Mansell, whose mood was not helped when Piquet won the race ahead of Senna. Mansell would come to rue the loss of potential points so early in the race and the season.

3
Laying Down a Marker

The potential folly of the first lap is drummed into every racing driver from an early age. Lewis Hamilton, having entered countless kart races, will not have needed reminding of the dangers inherent within a closely bunched group of machines fuelled by petrol in the engines and adrenalin coursing through the drivers' veins. Nonetheless, Hamilton will have been even more aware of the opportunities for advancement before the race settled down.

That will not have prevented mention being made of the perils of Melbourne's first corner. History showed that hardly a year went by without at least one car running on to the grass at the exit. If he was lucky, the driver would continue at the back of the field. Those less fortunate would be left to climb from wreckage and think of their excuses while making an unplanned arrival in the pits on foot.

The Red Bulletin, a lavishly produced daily publication that acts rather like an upmarket school magazine for F1 at every Grand Prix, carried a feature entitled '20 reasons why there will be a pile-up at the first corner'. Reason number 13 in this tongue-in-cheek piece said: 'SUPERIORITY. "We have no number one, our drivers have equal status" = matching drivers, matching cars, matching grudges – and one racing line.' Number 4 said: 'EXPERIENCE. The grid has rookies at the front, in the middle and at the back. If that isn't a recipe for shredded carbon fibre, what is?' With Hamilton on the second row, Heikki Kovalainen's first appearance in a Renault on row seven and Adrian Sutil making his debut in a Spyker on row eleven at the back, it was a fair question.

Hamilton had Alonso directly ahead on the front row. With pole position earning the advantage of the clean side of the track, Kimi Räikkönen would start his Ferrari on the racing line, on the left. The McLarens would line up on the right, which might not be a serious disadvantage because, given a reasonable getaway, Alonso and Hamilton could be in a good position when arriving at the first corner, a ninety-degree right-hander. On the other hand, Hamilton would need to apply caution in such a tight situation. It would be a shame if his F1 career literally got off to a bad start.

Such a thought seemed to be far from his mind as Hamilton found himself boxed in by Robert Kubica, who had started alongside the McLaren. Rather than sit tight, Hamilton lifted his foot from the throttle momentarily and ducked behind the white BMW. Not only did he then draw alongside Kubica on the left, Hamilton also had the advantage of Alonso as the track immediately swung left into the second corner. As the field began to emerge from turn 2, Hamilton found himself in third place, hard on the heels of Räikkönen's leading Ferrari and the fast-starting BMW of Nick Heidfeld.

If ever there was a marker for the season ahead, then this was it. As far as Hamilton was concerned, bravado did not enter into the equation. This was simply a racing situation at the first corner, something he had experienced a thousand times at countless different racetracks around the world. Hamilton had seen a gap and he had gone for it. Simple. He did what came naturally. 'I couldn't believe how early some of the drivers braked for the first corner,' Hamilton would say later. Those drivers probably could not believe how late Hamilton had braked and doubtless some might have thought he was fortunate to get away with it.

As the forthcoming races would show, luck would play no part in audacious but perfectly judged moves such as this.

Alonso's assessment of his new team-mate must have changed substantially in the short time it took McLaren's number two to suddenly appear alongside at the exit of turn 1 and then enjoy the positional advantage as they accelerated through the next corner. Alonso was powerless to respond, a feeling he would become painfully familiar with as the seventeen-race season followed its course. On this occasion, Alonso would benefit from a tactical advantage presented to him by the team as the race unfolded. But it was not until the second and final pit stop had been played out that the Spaniard actually got ahead.

For 50 minutes, Alonso had been forced to follow Hamilton and note the absence of serious errors despite this being such a landmark occasion for the novice. Hamilton was under serious pressure but he appeared to be soaking it up. Alonso, by not pushing to move ahead, was cleverly saving fuel while running in his team-mate's slipstream, a move which would allow him to run longer and, eventually, faster in the middle phase of the race and ensure he was able to move ahead after the second stop.

By the time the McLaren drivers joined Räikkönen on the podium, Alonso was now aware of the serious challenge from within his own team. Despite the smiles and backslapping, the rot had already begun to corrode McLaren's carefully managed modus operandi from within. But, as events would later prove, Alonso's disquiet would not be the most serious source of damage to McLaren's immaculate image.

McLaren's immediate concern was to address the dominant performance of the Ferrari. Räikkönen had won, more or less as he pleased, and Felipe Massa might have been right with him had a gearbox problem during qualifying not relegated the other Ferrari to sixteenth on the grid. Statistics showed the McLarens and the rest to be significantly slower than Räikkönen when running fresh tyres and a full load of fuel. But, F1 being such a hotbed of suspicion, there had been talk in the Melbourne paddock of Ferrari managing to bend the rules without actually breaking them.

The final performance of a F1 car is governed largely by the passage of air over and under it. These laws of aerodynamics dictate that the lower the car runs to the ground, the faster it will go. There are myriad restrictions imposed by the technical regulations, one of which prohibits certain parts of the bodywork from moving in order to gain a performance advantage. The floor of a F1 car is a critical area and it was believed that Ferrari had incorporated a clever spring fastener that allowed the floor of their car to flex more than it should when at speed, but which was perfectly legal when measured while the car was stationary. Rather than protest, McLaren asked the sport's governing body, the FIA, for a clarification about whether or not they could run a similar system in the future. The FIA were quick to issue a revision to their technical regulations that called for a tougher flexibility test, thus ruling out the use of the sprung floor. That seemed to be that.

McLaren (and others) had spotted the exploitation of a loophole that had now been closed. At the time, McLaren's actions were put down to the credible fact that engineers study their rivals' cars intently and McLaren's educated guesswork over the Ferrari floor had been proved correct. That view would change dramatically four months later. In the meantime, far greater importance was being attached to the actual racing and the remarkable progress of Lewis Hamilton.

A podium finish in his first race was more than Hamilton could wish for. He talked about 'living the dream'. Whether that would become a nightmare depended on how he got on as the scene shifted to Malaysia and Sepang, another track that was unfamiliar to Hamilton. His disappointment with fourth fastest qualifying time said as much about the expectation encouraged during his debut as it did about the reality check provided by the three drivers ahead of him, one of whom was Alonso in the other McLaren.

Qualifying at Sepang was never likely to be straightforward for an experienced campaigner, never mind a novice beginning to live with the relentless demands of a seventeen-race season. The 3.44-mile track, the third longest on the calendar with every conceivable type of corner, is one of the most difficult to come to terms with. Hamilton seemed to have a handle on Sepang but a sprinkling of rain in the closing minutes of qualifying brought an understandable touch of caution as he set off on his final lap. He said:

> There were a few spots of rain at one point on the circuit and I didn't know how hard I could push. That was enough to make the difference. But it's all part of the learning experi-ence I am going through between now and the end of the season. On the one hand, I'm a little disappointed but, on the other, I didn't make any mistakes and fourth on the grid isn't too bad. The important point is that Ferrari are not as far ahead of us as they were in Melbourne and we don't know what strategy they are running for the race.

Massa snatched pole position from Räikkönen. Alonso then split the two Ferraris with a lap that was 0.6 seconds faster than Hamilton and exacerbated the Englishman's mild frustration. Hamilton's mention of strategy was a reference to Massa having perhaps qualified his Ferrari with less fuel on board in order to claim his fourth pole position but then pay a penalty by making an early first stop to refuel (drivers had to qualify with the same amount of fuel that they intended to carry for the first phase of the race).

While Massa may have given Räikkönen something to think about, Alonso continued to establish the expected pecking order within McLaren by reading the conditions perfectly and producing faultless laps when they mattered. This would be a tough test for Hamilton. With the ambient temperature constantly hovering around 35 degrees C, this combined with 50 per cent humidity would make the 56-lap race the most physically demanding on the calendar. It was another drive into unknown territory; would Hamilton be able to cope with conditions that can cause drivers to lose as much as 10 kilogrammes during 90 minutes of intense concentration and physical effort?

That seemed of no consequence when the two Ferraris and two McLarens raced towards the first corner. Any questions about Hamilton having been lucky at the start in Melbourne were quickly dismissed when he pulled off an even more impressive move at Sepang – aided, it has to be said, by the Ferrari drivers appearing to fall asleep.

Massa started the disastrous sequence by leaving room on the inside as the leaders approached the first corner, a right-hander, Alonso needing no second bidding to snatch the lead. Hamilton could hardly believe his luck when Räikkönen did exactly the same thing; the Englishman duplicated the actions of his teammate a few yards ahead. But Hamilton was not yet finished. The second corner, a left-hander, followed immediately after the first. By running round the outside of Massa at the left-hander, Hamilton was perfectly positioned to take the line through the next corner and demote Massa to third. Once again, Hamilton had gone racing. He had seen a gap – two, in fact – and used them to his advantage. Now the world began to sit up and take notice. So far, so good. There were 55 laps to run.

Massa was not about to let the moment pass without retaliation. Pushing the McLaren hard on lap 4, Massa went for a gap on the inside as they approached turn 4. Hamilton saw him coming, but judged that Massa had been too adventurous. Sure enough, the Ferrari got alongside and then ran wide at the exit of the right-hander. On lap 6, Massa tried again at the same place.

This time Hamilton left slightly less room on his right and braked as late as he dared. Massa fell for it, braked impossibly late and ran on to the grass on the outside of the corner. Hamilton calmly continued on his way, doubtless with a broad grin after enjoying such a good scrap with the Brazilian.

With the Ferraris falling behind and Alonso driving superbly at the front, Hamilton focused on consolidating second place. Everything seemed perfectly under control when he set the fastest lap of the race but, inside the baking-hot cockpit, Hamilton was alarmed to discover that he had used up his drinks supply. There were 20 laps remaining – and Räikkönen was closing fast. This would be yet another test. Would Hamilton crack under the Finn's relentless pressure in such torrid conditions?

Digging deep into his physical and mental reserves, Hamilton did not put a wheel out of place despite the Ferrari closing to within a car's length in the final stages. Second place and another podium was one thing but, on the cooling down lap, Hamilton got on the radio and calmly told his engineer, Phil Prew, 'I really think a win will come.' This was not an idle boast and yet it was necessary to remind yourself that he had completed just two F1 races.

It took Nigel Mansell seventy-two Grands Prix before he won his first. It was part of the character-building process that made Mansell such a gritty competitor, a driver who would bounce back despite having ended the first race of 1986 against the crash barrier. The next round was at Jerez in Spain, where Mansell waged a tense battle with Senna, the Englishman having made a late stop for fresh tyres. With 8 laps to go, Mansell was third, 19 seconds behind Senna. As they started the last lap, he was second, just 1.5 seconds behind the Lotus. They crossed the line with Mansell drawing alongside, Senna taking the victory by 0.014 seconds.

For this race, the finishing line had been moved from near the

Chequered Conflict

end of the pit straight to its beginning. Had the timing beam remained in its original position, Mansell would have been ahead and won. In 1986, points were awarded 9, 6, 4, 3, 2 and 1 to the first six finishers. Those extra 3 points would have made a huge difference to Mansell at the end of the season. As Lewis Hamilton was to discover twenty-one years later, it is the small details that count when F1 is as competitive as this.

4
Alonso in the Dirt

The Sakhir paddock has the atmosphere of an immaculate industrial estate rather than a place of world championship sporting endeavour. Introduced to the calendar in 2004, the Bahrain Grand Prix was a clean and crisp sign of the way the sport was heading, probably at the expense of some if its more traditional venues such as Monza and Spa-Francorchamps, places that would find it increasingly difficult to raise the necessary cash to meet F1's demands.

Bahrain was built at a cost of £100 million, the Royal Family and government lending their full support to a project that would bring F1 to the Gulf region for the first time and enhance the country's image. The facilities were first class. Each team had the use of a fitted stainless-steel kitchen; a major step forward for catering crews normally accustomed on long-haul races to struggling with a portable gas hob in a partitioned area within the team's temporary cabin. The meeting rooms were air-conditioned, each had a shower, and a toilet; one for the boys and one for the girls, which made a change from queuing at an overworked Portaloo such as those positioned in the paddock in Montreal. The media enjoyed the use of free Internet piped to each desk within a press centre that seemed almost as big as the paddocks at more elderly venues such as Imola in Italy.

The problem was that creature comforts had become more important than the track itself and, by definition, the quality of the racing. Sakhir is a shorter version of Sepang, but without the fast sections that make the Malaysian track so popular. The mystery was that more sweeping curves and undulations had not been incorporated in a region that was hardly short of space. Sakhir's only limitation was on the south side of the track where an ancient burial ground had obvious precedence over the efforts of those trying to breathe new life into F1 and Bahrain.

The circuit is a bland collection of standard corners linked by straights. According to the drivers, it is technically quite tricky to master. But, as one of the world's breathtaking challenges to man and machine, this circuit fell a long way short, particularly as most of it was laid out behind the pits in a desert from which spectators were banned. That did not matter to the sport's power brokers and managers, the majority of whom never left the pit lane and paddock and could only view the impressive grandstand opposite. Their world was a tidy oasis of calm devoid of the clutter of tyres and equipment normally spread around a more traditional working area behind the garages. Palm trees, allegedly at £1000 each, had been positioned with seating at regular intervals along the centre of the massive concrete paddock to provide shade from the searing heat.

On Thursday, 12 April 2007, Fernando Alonso and Ron Dennis took refuge on a bench while holding a lengthy conversation. The photo opportunity was not to be missed and the pair were soon surrounded at a discreet distance by the sound of whirring motor drives. Whether or not Dennis was deliberately using this public place to emphasize his willingness to chat to his driver did not matter; it was clear that a serious conversation was taking place with Dennis doing most of the talking. The season may have been a mere two races old but the McLaren boss was already aware of the double world champion's disquiet. Dennis, sensitive to any suggestion that one driver was being favoured over the other, had noted that Alonso had been mildly irritated at the team's post-qualifying press conference in

Melbourne when nearly all of the questions had been directed at Hamilton even though he, Alonso, had been the faster of the two. Alonso had since gone on to score a dominant win in Malaysia but Dennis nevertheless felt the need to grab the opportunity on their day of arrival in Bahrain and provide reassurance.

'We were just talking about a couple of things, life in general,' said Dennis, when quizzed about the tête-à-tête. 'It was a slightly paternal approach. We are trying to manage the drivers, keeping their feet on the ground and making sure everyone knows we are privileged to have a double world champion in our car.'

It was the first public sign that there might be trouble brewing within McLaren. Alonso was keen to use his champion status to gain leverage within a team that he knew would insist on treating both drivers the same. More important, Alonso was quickly becoming aware that Hamilton would be more than capable of using his equal opportunity, possibly at the Spaniard's expense. Dennis's chat appeared not to have provided the necessary reassurance, particularly when Alonso later told Spanish journalists that he felt his boss had been patronizing when explaining their conversation to the media.

Matters were not helped on the track. Alonso never looked completely at home as he struggled to become accustomed to the brakes required for Sakhir. This track, along with Montreal, placed the highest demands on the ability of the car to remain stable and sensitive when going from 190 m.p.h. to 50 m.p.h. in less than two seconds on at least three parts of the circuit. In between, there was little opportunity for the brakes to cool, thus calling for a hard-wearing brake material that Alonso found difficulty coping with but which, significantly, Hamilton, who had no preconceived ideas about how different F1 brakes should work, could manage easily. When Hamilton was faster in qualifying and therefore had first call on the best pit stop strategy in the race, Alonso's disaffection was compounded.

Hamilton qualified second fastest and knew immediately that

his major rival would be Massa. The Brazilian, having come under criticism for his performance a week before, had taken pole position and was keen to right the wrongs of Malaysia. It would be a test of Massa's temperament under pressure. He went to the grid knowing that he would be savaged by the Italian media if he were seen to throw away another potential victory with a silly mistake.

In the event, Massa drove a perfect race. Hamilton applied pressure in the early stage but the Ferrari driver did not flinch. When Hamilton had a problem with the pressures on his second set of tyres, Massa made his escape and crossed the line with a recovering Hamilton (on a correctly inflated third set of tyres) just 0.2 seconds behind.

Räikkönen was third in the other Ferrari. If Räikkönen's race had not been particularly inspiring, then Alonso's was less so. Clearly lacking confidence in his brakes, a major setback on a circuit such as this, Alonso suffered the additional indignity of being pushed down to fifth place thanks to an audacious passing move by the BMW of Nick Heidfeld. After three races, the two McLaren drivers each had 22 points, making Hamilton the joint leader of the world championship.

Having left Britain as a relative unknown six weeks before, Hamilton returned as Britain's new sporting hero. He arrived at his home in Hertfordshire to find at least ten journalists and photographers camped outside his parents' house. The life of the 22-year-old had changed irrevocably thanks to setting a record for a F1 novice by finishing on the podium in his first three Grands Prix. There was a genuine expectation that he could win his first Grand Prix at the next round in Spain. But not if Alonso had his way.

Stung by such a drubbing at the hands of a novice in Bahrain, Alonso persuaded the McLaren management to allow him to do the pre-race testing at Barcelona, along with McLaren's test driver, fellow-Spaniard Pedro de la Rosa. Alonso wished to learn more about the car and the Bridgestone tyres. He also wanted to try the McLaren's latest modifications at the expense of Hamilton, who was excluded from the test. Not that it mattered.

When practice began, Hamilton was faster than Alonso in the first session. Alonso was stunned. More than anything, this doubled his resolve to claim pole position. To do that, he would need to run with a light load of fuel in the third and final sector of qualifying (known as 'Q3'). If he could wedge at least one of the Ferraris between himself and Hamilton, then Alonso could make good his escape, stop early, still retain the lead, and win the race.

The plan would have worked except for one thing: Alonso did not take into account an extraordinary lap from Massa at the very end of qualifying. Alonso would start from second on the grid, with Räikkönen third and Hamilton fourth. When Alonso came to a halt in the pit lane, his arrival was greeted in comparative silence by the Spanish faithful, a stark contrast to the scene of near-hysteria in 2006 when the world champion stood on his Renault and welcomed the adulation after destroying the opposition during qualifying. This time, Alonso was more bemused than bothered. Having committed to running with low fuel, one thing was clear: Alonso simply *had* to get ahead of Massa at the start.

As the leaders approached the first corner, Alonso tried to run round the outside of the Ferrari but Massa refused to be intimidated. The two cars touched, sending the McLaren across the kerb and into the dirt. By the time Alonso had regained the track, he had been passed by a McLaren and a Ferrari, Hamilton tweaking Alonso's total frustration by having passed Räikkönen on the way into the corner. Now Lewis was second and Alonso was fourth. And Alonso could blame no one but himself as Massa took his second win in succession ahead of Hamilton. The only luck coming Alonso's way was an engine failure for Räikkönen that allowed the home hero into third place.

Chequered Conflict

After four races, Hamilton led the championship to become the youngest driver to do so in the history of the sport. It was somehow appropriate that Hamilton had taken the record from Bruce McLaren, the founder of his team. McLaren had been one month older when he set the record in 1960. Hamilton was twenty-two years, four months and six days old. Alonso must suddenly have felt even older than his modest twenty-five years. This was becoming increasingly difficult for the Spaniard to take.

Until his arrival at McLaren, Alonso had always managed to dominate his team-mate. On the rare occasions when Giancarlo Fisichella had the measure of Alonso during their partnership at Renault, Alonso's mask of cool respectability would slip to reveal sometimes irrational behaviour. Now there was the previously unimagined threat of self-doubt taking permanent hold as Hamilton proved to be at least Alonso's equal after just four races, an extraordinary feat considering the experience accumulated by Alonso during ninety-two Grands Prix.

The next three races in Monaco, Canada and the United States would be critical for Alonso. Hamilton may not have been familiar with either Montreal or Indianapolis but he was going to North America knowing that Alonso had hit the wall at the former (when in a fit of pique over Fisichella's progress in 2005) and he had a mental block over the latter, never having finished higher than fifth. Speaking on his team's official podcast, Renault's team manager Steve Nielsen summed up Alonso's potential difficulties: 'In his career, Fernando has always been comfortably faster than team-mates, and now he's got a guy who's his equal, if not maybe a little bit quicker in the races, as we've seen so far. I think he'll be questioning himself, deep down inside, as to whether he is really quicker than his team-mate. The few times we saw Fernando really under pressure were when his team-mate beat him. That's the situation he's in now.'

And Monaco, one of the trickiest races on the calendar, was next.

5

Big Casino in
Monte Carlo

ewis Hamilton went to Monaco knowing he had won three times before (twice in Formula Three and once in GP2). He loved the circuit and its unique challenges and he was not put off in the slightest by a heavy meeting with the crash barrier during the opening day of practice. This was his first public mistake but Hamilton adopted the attitude: 'these things happen'. Here was another box waiting to be ticked. A fast lap at Monaco requires the driver to have confidence in himself and his machinery. He has to take that car to the limit, and sometimes beyond as the wheel rims make a musical sing-song while kissing the steel barriers. Get it right and the lap looks and feels sensational. Get it wrong and the resulting damage affects not just the car's suspension but the driver's self-assurance. Hamilton appeared not to have given the earlier incident a second thought as he focused on winning pole position despite carrying 5 laps more fuel than Alonso during Q3, the final phase of qualifying.

In theory, the extra weight should have held Hamilton back. In reality, the only thing holding Hamilton back had been the Red Bull of Mark Webber as Hamilton tried to complete his final and fastest lap. Amazingly, Hamilton had been 0.35 seconds faster than Alonso halfway round that lap. Then he came across Webber, who was returning to the pits. The tight confines of the street circuit meant Hamilton was delayed enough to lose pole by 0.2 seconds. Hamilton was annoyed but put on a brave face because he knew he had more fuel on board and could overtake Alonso by running longer at the time of the first pit stop. That was the theory. The reality would turn out to be different. Team tactics, run for the right reasons, were about to send relationships down the start of a slippery slope from which recovery would be impossible.

Mindful of the need to avoid a collision at the first corner, and despite making a slightly better start than Alonso, Hamilton dutifully slotted behind his team-mate, the better to defend them both from an attack by Massa's Ferrari. That done, Hamilton knew the superior pace of the McLaren was such that he could focus totally on his race. And that was a good feeling because Hamilton also knew, all things being equal, he was in a strong position.

Except that all things were not equal. Once Alonso had made his first stop, McLaren only allowed Hamilton another 3 laps before calling him in. Instead of having 5 laps to get round Monaco over a second a lap faster than the now fuel-heavy Alonso, Hamilton felt he was being short-changed by being brought in early. He rejoined behind Alonso, knowing his chance had been shot and wondering why he had been handicapped by extra weight during qualifying but was unable to use the advantage those additional pre-stop laps could have brought him for the race. McLaren would later claim that the advantage would have accrued to Hamilton had there been a Safety Car period, the extra fuel allowing him greater flexibility. In the event, surprisingly so for Monaco, the Safety Car was never needed as the drivers behaved themselves and raced without incident.

Concerned that the McLarens might run out of brakes if the leaders continued at their breakneck pace, Hamilton was asked to reduce speed after his second stop. It was the first time in his racing career that Hamilton had been told to go slowly when he felt he had the speed to win. He did not like it. Hamilton later said he ignored that instruction and pushed hard, knowing that the only way he might overtake at Monaco would be through Alonso making a mistake – 'but twice world champions rarely make mistakes – and there weren't any from Fernando'. Such was the speed of the McLarens, they lapped the entire field with the exception of Massa in a distant third place.

None of the frustration of the early pit stop came to light until Hamilton was asked about it at the post-race press conference. He did not mince his words. 'It says number 2 on my car, so I guess I'm the number 2 driver,' was the clipped reply. Alonso, sitting alongside, did not look amused. Ron Dennis, watching the press conference piped into the McLaren offices, knew instantly that there was trouble looming. Sure enough, within minutes of the conference finishing, a posse of British media was beating a path to Dennis's door to ask why their hero had been denied the chance of victory.

Dennis tried to explain the significance of a possible Safety Car period compromising a very important one–two finish for the team if the second stopping car (Hamilton) had not made his pit visit when the Safety Car appeared. In such an instance, there would have been the strong possibility that Hamilton would have become stuck behind drivers stopping just once when the field became bunched behind the official car. The argument, logical as it was from a no-risk, conservative point of view, fell on ground made barren by the fact the Safety Car had never appeared, thus apparently rendering this tactical argument irrelevant in the eyes of those who wished to trumpet a British victory rather than grapple with F1's sometimes complicated strategies.

Hamilton, meanwhile, continued to leave no doubt that this could have been his first victory. The subsequent outcry in the British media was enough to prompt the sport's governing body to launch an inquiry into McLaren's tactics but the FIA would come away satisfied with McLaren's reasoning. Alonso, meanwhile, felt Hamilton's public airing of what should have been a private tactical matter for the team had demeaned a faultless performance throughout the weekend (Hamilton had crashed during practice and touched the barrier during the race whereas Alonso's car had remained completely unmarked throughout). That could not disguise the fact that, of the two McLaren drivers, Hamilton had been potentially the faster, during both qualifying and the race. Now they were joint leaders of the championship on 38 points. Massa had 33; Räikkönen was on 23. Just five races in and the Finn was being discounted by many as having no chance of winning the championship.

Räikkönen had finished eighth after a small but disastrous error during qualifying. This seemed to sum up the Finn's struggle after coming from McLaren and Michelin tyres to Ferrari and the standard Bridgestone that every team used in 2007 following the withdrawal of Michelin. Räikkönen was having difficulty setting up the Ferrari to his liking, a handicap at a place such as Monaco where a driver needs precision of mind and motor as he attacks the narrow streets. During the first phase of qualifying when the leading runners were under the least amount of pressure, Räikkönen had managed to smack the barrier at the apex of a corner where the track skirts the harbour-side swimming pool. That elementary mistake relegated the Ferrari to sixteenth on the grid. Räikkönen may not have been satisfied with a solid drive into eighth place but that single championship point would mean everything when the final day of reckoning arrived. It was shaping up to be that sort of championship but there were few in Monaco who would have bet on Räikkönen winning it.

6

A Safer Way of Getting Hurt

The Monaco track gives the impression of having remained more or less the same since its inception in 1929. It is true that the snaking uphill dash from Sainte Devote and the sweeping turns between the magnificent facades of the Casino and the Hotel de Paris have not altered any more than the subsequent steep drop through Mirabeau and on towards to the waterfront. But beyond Portier corner, certain parts have been changed, some more dramatically than others.

In 1986, the Automobile Club de Monaco publicized the fact that almost £1 million had been required to pay for modifications made necessary by the need to tailor the track to suit the latest cars. The argument that this might be a case of the tail wagging the dog was dismissed as ignorance of the need for progress. A fast chicane leading on to the harbour side had been deemed too quick, the left–right flick giving way to a more pedestrian left-hander followed by a right leading on to the quay. To achieve this, the Monégasques had to pile the harbour and graft a concrete extension on to the quayside, there being no alternative to go inland because of a sheer rock face on the inside of the track. Drivers were not enamoured with the stuttering first and second gear corners that resulted. However, this was what was needed to keep speeds in check and Monaco on the calendar.

It was thought that the new chicane would at least provide a much-needed overtaking point after the 175-m.p.h. dash through the tunnel but this did not prove to be the case in 1986, one of the many signs that this race had hardly been enthralling. To say that the procession was headed by Prost from beginning to end would be to understate the Frenchman's brilliance. He did not dominate simply by preventing others from overtaking; he scored his second win in as many weeks by taking an impressive pole position and then disappearing into a world of his own for the best part of two hours. The closest anyone got to the McLaren driver was when being lapped. It marked a turnaround for Prost and moved him to within 2 points of the joint championship leaders, Senna and Piquet. Mansell, yet to really get into his stride, was fourth, 7 points behind Prost. All of that would change within the next two weeks. In fact, motor sport in general and F1 in particular was about to receive a shock to the system.

When Mansell climbed on to the top step of the podium at Spa-Francorchamps two weeks later, there was hardly the flicker of a smile. The Englishman was experiencing both ends of the motor racing spectrum in Belgium as his first win of the season was tinged with great sadness. A few days before, Elio de Angelis had been fatally injured during a test session at the Paul Ricard circuit. Mansell and de Angelis had been team-mates during difficult days at Lotus and the Englishman was affected more than most by the first F1-related fatality since 1982. Racing drivers knew and accepted that risk was part of the job. What appalled everyone gathered at Spa for the Belgian Grand Prix was that de Angelis appeared to have died needlessly.

The irony was that de Angelis disliked testing. The modest Italian preferred to rely on an abundance of talent and car control to do the job but a disappointing performance at Monaco, where he had qualified at the back of the grid, prompted a visit to the test track in France. De Angelis was driving for Brabham-BMW, a team that was not enjoying a competitive season with a distinctive low-line car that had the driver almost flat on his back. The driving position had nothing to do with an accident caused by a rear wing failure as de Angelis approached the 180-m.p.h. Verrerie S-bend. With no rear downforce forcing the Brabham on to the track, the car took off, cleared the crash barrier and landed upside-down on the inside of the circuit. De Angelis suffered nothing more than a broken collarbone. That may have been a fitting tribute to the strength of the car but it highlighted the scandal of what happened next.

Alan Jones, also testing that day, stopped his Lola-Ford and ran to the overturned car, which had now caught fire with the driver trapped inside. The 1980 world champion was appalled to find only two marshals on hand and with no equipment to help right the car. Jones was soon joined by Prost and Mansell but, even allowing for their flameproof driving suits, they were prevented by the heat from getting close enough to help. When a fire marshal eventually arrived, he was wearing a T-shirt and shorts and carrying an inadequate extinguisher. Jones noted that most of the powder was directed into the cockpit rather than on the fire.

It was ten minutes before de Angelis could be extracted. There was no helicopter on standby and it took another thirty minutes for one to arrive from Marseilles. De Angelis was transferred to hospital but, twenty-four hours later, he was pronounced dead due to 'head and chest injuries'. Jones was not alone in believing that de Angelis had suffered brain injury thanks to asphyxiation.

There was an immediate knee-jerk reaction from Jean-Marie Balestre, the president of the sport's governing body, then known as FISA. Balestre called for a reduction in engine power and demanded that the Verrerie S-bend be removed from the forthcoming French Grand Prix by cutting the circuit in two. None of this addressed the more vital problem of inadequate marshalling.

During a Grand Prix weekend, a car would not be allowed to turn a wheel unless there were at least four marshals at every corner, supported by rescue vehicles and an attendant helicopter.

Chequered Conflict

In 1986, testing was manned by the minimum number of staff at some, but not all, of the circuits, as if to suggest that any accident would somehow be less serious because the drivers were not actually racing. Each team had paid £800 for the day's testing in France and, as one team manager pointed out, 'for that sort of money you naturally expect the circuit organizers to have provided the necessary services'. The de Angelis tragedy, the last to occur in F1 until the death of Roland Ratzenberger and Ayrton Senna in 1994, was to prompt a major overhaul of safety facilities. Today, a test session will not commence unless, at the very least, it has the back up found at a Grand Prix.

There had been an adequate number of marshals on hand at Spa on the day Mansell won. Senna had finished second and Piquet, starting from pole, had retired from the lead with turbo trouble after 16 of the 43 laps. If Piquet felt he should have won this race, then so did Prost, who came home sixth. Starting directly behind Piquet's Williams, Prost found himself squeezed to the inside of a very tight hairpin as three cars tried to run side-by-side through the first corner. Unable to avoid the moment, Prost locked wheels with Gerhard Berger's Benetton before becoming airborne briefly and crashing nose-first on to the kerbing on the outside of the corner. Prost managed to limp back to the pits for a new nose on the McLaren before rejoining in twenty-third place.

Prost, one of the most sensitive drivers of his generation, knew the car did not feel right, but pressed on regardless at one of the fastest and most daunting tracks in the world. It was to be a truly magnificent comeback drive made even more amazing when it was discovered that his McLaren had bent engine mountings and damaged suspension. John Barnard, McLaren's technical chief, was stunned when he examined Prost's car after the race. 'The top right-hand engine plate [which attached the engine to the back of the chassis] was bent like a banana,' said Barnard. 'You can't bend one engine plate and leave the rest straight. The whole engine must have been skewed which means his car was literally bent in the middle. How he went as fast as he did, I just don't know. Absolutely incredible.' Prost somehow managed to set the fastest lap of the race, a full half a second faster than anyone else, a heroic effort that produced a single point for sixth place. It did not seem much at the time but, like Räikkönen at Monaco twenty-one years later, Prost would discover that little things could mean a lot.

Mansell could reflect on the same thing when considering how his pit crew had helped him win with a very slick stop to change tyres (refuelling was not allowed). The Williams team had Mansell away in 7.9 seconds; very fast in 1986; very slow in 2007. The return of refuelling in 1994, following a ten year ban, would encourage teams to raise the business of pit stops to new heights. The crews were efficient in 1986 with two, sometimes three mechanics per wheel, a jack man front and rear and usually the team manager standing at the front ready to beckon the driver to leave. Since fuel was not involved, they would be wearing cotton shirts and shorts.

In 2007, McLaren would have twenty-three people, smothered from head to foot in flame-proof gear and helmets, perform a beautifully orchestrated movement as four tyres were changed in as many seconds and up to 70 litres of fuel added by the time the clock had reached 7 seconds, sometimes less. Pit stops – or, more important, their planning – were to play a huge part in Lewis Hamilton's race when the scene shifted to round six in Canada.

7

Hamilton Beyond Doubt

The Circuit Gilles Villeneuve is popular for reasons other than its location on an island in the middle of the St Lawrence River. The island has been made from the construction waste produced by an underground railway that serves it. The track, a short Metro ride from Montreal's city centre, runs along the island's perimeter road. A limited number of cars are allowed within the circuit's boundary.

The main source of congestion is people, close to 100,000 knowledgeable and enthusiastic fans adding to an excellent atmosphere. The circuit is flat and punctuated by five chicanes, an unappetizing combination on paper but one that regularly produces plenty of drama because the cars run with minimum downforce in search of straight-line speed. The downside is that the cars lack grip, particularly when braking from high speed. Errors are often punished spectacularly by walls lining a track that is bumpy in places thanks to the ravages of the Canadian winter.

The island was made for Expo 67 and used again in 1976 as a location for the Olympic rowing lake, which now forms a unique backdrop to the paddock. There can be no better way of arriving at work than by a motorboat plying its way through water dappled by early morning sunshine. Most F1 personnel travel by car, entry to the paddock being gained on foot via a temporary pontoon crossing the lake, a wobbly means of access that can indicate publicly your stability after the night before.

Chequered Conflict

There is much to entertain the drivers in the city at night. Hamilton will have enjoyed none of this as he arrived in Montreal, keen to learn a track he had not seen before. More than anything, he wanted pole. After the upset in Monaco, the Englishman knew this was one way of ensuring there could be no question about which McLaren driver would be in a position to win the race. That was assuming, of course, that the Circuit Gilles Villeneuve would suit the McLaren-Mercedes better than the Ferrari. In 2007, you never knew which team would gain the impetus until practice got under way. With five races gone, the only certainty was that the fight would be between these two teams.

One of the keys to a fast lap in Montreal is the ability of a car to ride the kerbs that mark the chicanes. The McLaren's capacity to soak up the bumps would suit Hamilton perfectly. The Ferraris were struggling. Now all he had to do was make his car work better than Alonso's.

After free practice on Friday, Hamilton knew the track was not as straightforward as it seemed. 'The layout looks simple enough,' he said. 'But it's a real challenge – physical, mental and technical.' He returned to his hotel to ponder where the odd one tenth of a second could be found over the circuit's 2.71 miles. Small changes to the set-up of the McLaren worked perfectly on Saturday morning. By the time he was ready for qualifying, Hamilton described the car as feeling 'sweet'.

He proved it by taking his first pole position with a lap that he truly believed he could not have done any quicker. 'I came through the final corner faster than I had gone before,' said Hamilton. 'When they tell you on the radio that you've won pole, it's the greatest feeling in the world.' To make the moment even sweeter – not that Hamilton would have mentioned it – he had been assisted by Alonso making a mistake when he ran wide at the hairpin on a lap, which, until that point, had been the fastest of all. Now Hamilton had to convert this pole position into his first victory. Once again, Alonso would inadvertently help him on his way. Going into the first corner, the Spaniard took to the grass on the outside while trying to keep Heidfeld's BMW out of second place. The track then went from left to right and Alonso shot back on to the road, straight across Hamilton's bows. Hamilton recalled:

> I made quite a poor getaway, to be honest. I don't know what exactly happened but the revs were too high. I saw Nick getting close, so I had to close the door and cover my position. Then I saw Fernando fly past on my right. Obviously, I didn't want that. I thought: 'No! I'm going to lose it [the lead] here.' But somehow he went straight on. I just took the first corner as normal and got a fantastic exit from the second – and Fernando came flying across in front of me as he rejoined the track. That start was quite exciting and it was just great to get out in front because I knew it was my opportunity to go away, into the distance. I didn't know what happened to Fernando after that.

Alonso had dropped to third place and would make more mistakes before finishing a distant seventh. Now Hamilton had to focus on staying in front. There were to be plenty of distractions, but luck went Hamilton's way when he made his first pit stop after 22 laps, which happened to be shortly before the Safety Car appeared to deal with a crashed car. Alonso was due to stop on the next lap but the advent of the Safety Car meant he was now supposed to queue behind it until permitted to pit. (Safety Car periods usually invite a rash of pit stops at a moment when the drivers will lose the minimum of track time. Officials had become concerned about drivers rushing past the scene of the incident while desperate not to lose time on their way to the pits. A new rule in 2007 said that drivers were not permitted to enter the pits until they had lined up behind the Safety Car and were finally given the all clear to pit.) McLaren had run their fuel calculations to the limit, leaving them with no option but to bring Alonso in immediately and incur a ten-second penalty. It was either that or have him run out fuel. It was the luck of the draw, exactly the sort of thing McLaren had been anxious to avoid when they brought Hamilton into the pits earlier than planned at Monaco.

'The team did a great job getting me in before the first Safety Car appeared and I have to say that was a very good call, because I think that was earlier than I was supposed to stop,' said Hamilton. 'Quite a few people got caught out by the Safety Car. But I had made my stop and was out front, in the clean air. I was very fortunate.'

It would not be the last time Hamilton would see the rear end of the AMG Mercedes CLK Safety Car. Robert Kubica suffered an enormous accident when a misunderstanding with Jarno Trulli saw Kubica's BMW run into the back of the Toyota at 160 m.p.h. The impact dislodged Kubica's nose wing, which went under the front wheels, robbing him of steering and sending the BMW on to the grass and into the air. It hit the concrete wall on the right and launched into a terrifying series of barrel rolls, hit the wall once more and ricocheted from one side of the track to the other, shedding wheels and bodywork as it went before coming to a rest on its side, the driver showing no sign of life in the cockpit.

Kubica turned out to be mildly concussed but the violence of the accident had actually torn into the carbon fibre chassis and exposed his feet. It is the first time the latest breed of chassis had broken in this way. Cars must undergo massive impact tests before being allowed to race and the state of the front of the BMW said everything about the colossal force of the multiple impacts.

Professor Sid Watkins, the former FIA medical delegate who had been responsible for the introduction of a protective collar around the cockpit and the Hans device to which a driver's helmet is attached, had no doubt about what had saved Kubica from serious injury. 'We can say without much contradiction that the combination of the collar and the Hans device saved Robert's life,' said Watkins. 'If a driver had undergone such a violent accident ten years ago, there's no doubt he would have broken his neck. These two innovations have made a terrific contribution to safety in motor racing.'

Hamilton, meanwhile, had been concerned about Kubica, a driver whom he knew and liked after racing together in karts. He said:

I did not see the crash but there was a lot of debris all over the track. As I came past at first, I didn't focus on Robert's car because I was trying not to run over anything. I got to hear about Robert [from the team]. He's a good friend of mine and I was glad to learn that he was likely to be okay. People asked if this affected me. Not at all. I think the FIA have done a fantastic job by making safety the number one priority but everyone realizes that we always need to improve.

From my perspective, this meant another Safety Car period. Each time, your tyres get cold, your brakes get cold and it's so easy to start racing again and just put it in the wall. That was the real challenge: warming up your tyres enough and not making any mistakes.

Hamilton made no mistakes. Once the Safety Car had done its work and the field was released, Hamilton began to ease away from Heidfeld. Now he had to maintain concentration, avoid the tiny but treacherous pieces of rubber fringing the racing line and stay away from the walls. His race – his first win – could be gone in an instant. The concrete lining the outside of the final corner was known as 'The Champions' Wall' for good reason: many famous names had damaged cars and reputations against the unyielding barrier at the exit of this quick but tricky chicane. Hamilton said:

> The last few laps, I was just counting them down. I could see my board: four, three, two, one. I'm the type of guy who usually pushes right to the end but it's a tricky circuit and if you make one mistake, you get on the marbles [bits of rubber torn from the tyres] and you're in the wall. I was running slower and slower. It really was about just enjoying the whole moment. I was trying to control myself. I wanted to stop the car and jump out and just do, I don't know, cartwheels or something! I just had to keep it going.
>
> It was extremely emotional. It's really hard to grasp everything because it just keeps getting better and better. Firstly getting to Formula One, my first tests, becoming the Vodafone McLaren Mercedes race driver, having six podiums, my first pole in Canada, a circuit I had never seen before. Then my first win. I really did not think it would happen in Canada. The team gave me a fantastic car. I just had to knuckle down, keep focused and keep my mind clear – and that's what I did.

It was the British media's bad luck that the time difference between Montreal and the UK meant journalists were working to very tight deadlines. But that did not prevent sports editors from quickly scheming new back pages to mark this British victory. With just six races gone in 2007, no one was in any doubt that there would be more of the same from Lewis Carl Hamilton in the remaining eleven rounds.

8
In Search of Motown

Formula One has never taken root in the motor sport culture of the United States, which explains why this particular Grand Prix has had more homes than any other. From an airfield in Florida to the beautiful Watkins Glen racetrack in the Finger Lakes district of New York State; from the streets of Phoenix and Dallas to a bizarre location in a car park at the back of Caesar's Palace Hotel in Las Vegas: with the exception of Watkins Glen, none of these lasted longer than eight years, some staging the race just once. Temporary circuits were the most numerous and, of these, Long Beach in California and the streets of Detroit were the most popular. The latter would provide the venue for the United States Grand Prix in 1986.

When first mooted as a staging post for the race in 1982, Detroit had been considered something of a joke. The proposed track would run along the riverfront and through the fringe of the city's Downtown area. Even to the naked eye, the streets looked bumpy. At first glance, the layout seemed unimaginative as it followed the American street system of blocks to make the corners either a ninety-degree left or right, the circuit edges defined by pre-cast concrete walls dropped into place. But the quick bits in between, which included one or two curving sections near the river, were very fast indeed. The drivers, despite the anticipated complaints about bumps that would never be tolerated today, relished the challenge. And there were bonuses to be had when activity on the track had ceased.

The race quickly became popular with the local motor industry, the Ford Motor Company setting the pace with a lavish pre-event party in their magnificent museum in nearby Dearborn. The atmosphere at the track itself was instantly electric as the people of Michigan, and from Canada on the far side of the river, threw themselves into the business of partying in a manner matched only by the Australians. The race fans did not have to move far to find refreshment, the riverside straight being run in the shadow of the Renaissance Center. This glass-sided edifice, with its main tower stretching seventy-three floors, provided hotel rooms, office space, restaurants and bars. For those working in F1, getting to and from a racetrack has never been easier, either before or since.

It was not unreasonable to expect the drivers to attend press conferences in the media centre located within the Renaissance Center. After Friday's practice had finished, the fastest man, Mansell, got there in such indecent haste that he beat most of the journalists struggling to find the correct lift to take them to the appropriate floor. The following day, the reverse happened. In fact, the pole position man did not turn up at all.

Ayrton Senna was in his bedroom several floors up, preferring to watch Brazil play France in the World Cup rather than attend the post-action briefing which American writers in particular expected and enjoyed in other sports. Had this occurred in 2007, Senna would have been fined heavily by the FIA. But things were more relaxed at a time when press conferences were hit and miss and did not have the rigid and familiar scheduling imposed at every Grand Prix today. In 1986, the media had to make do with Senna's comments from a tape recorder held by a hapless and highly embarrassed PR lady from Lotus. The news that France had beaten Brazil was later received with some satisfaction by disgruntled F1 journalists who murmured it would be a shame if Brazil also lost this race.

There was a point when it looked as though that might happen. Senna, having seen off Mansell after the Englishman lost the lead with brake trouble on his Williams, then suffered a rear puncture and was forced to make an unscheduled pit stop after 12 laps. Senna had rushed into an area that would be unrecognizable as a pit lane today. Because of the track's temporary nature, the cars were garaged in Cobo Hall. This covered exhibition centre provided a luxurious working area by F1 standards, the only drawback being that it was at the far end of the circuit. Every last nut and bolt needed for running the cars during practice and the race had to be taken back and forth by van to the 'pits', which was nothing more than a lay-by on the waterfront. Once the track was closed for racing and a team discovered a vital piece of equipment had been left in Cobo Hall, then too bad. On one such occasion, the Tyrrell team tried dispatching a mechanic to make his way to the garage by pick-up truck. The man took a wrong turning and found himself in the tunnel, heading for Canada – and without his passport. Unless garages were built in the style of those introduced at Monaco a few years ago, Detroit would be completely unworkable today because of the banks of computers and the army of technicians necessary to operate them. But, in 1986, the most sophisticated piece of pit kit was an airgun to remove wheel nuts, followed closely by a cooler for soft drinks.

The Lotus crew had Senna under way in 11.7 seconds. During that time seven cars had gone by; among them, the Williams of Piquet. The Brazilian took the lead until it was time to come in for fresh Goodyears. The pit stop was scheduled, not so the problem with a sticking right-front wheel. Piquet was delayed for 18 seconds, Mansell having had an identical problem not long before. Senna, meanwhile, was in the middle of a mighty comeback drive, the black Lotus-Renault darting and dancing on the bumps as he carved through the field. A stop for more tyres on lap 40 had him under way in 8.2 seconds – and back in the lead.

Chequered Conflict

Piquet, realizing this would happen, had gone flat out from the moment he had rejoined. He set the fastest lap on lap 41, almost a full second quicker than anyone else. Then he crashed. Spectacularly.

Turning into the final left-hander before the pits, Piquet clipped the wall, the impact throwing the Williams across the track where, in full view of team members in the pits, he smacked the outside wall and destroyed the right-front suspension of the car.

Now began a comedy of errors, commonplace at the time. The hobbled Williams was stuck at the exit of a blind corner and needed to be removed quickly. The marshals engaged in much arm waving and whistle blowing, as is the tendency in North America, but to little effect. After 4 laps, the yellow warning flags disappeared. Assuming the wreck had been removed, Senna took his normal line through the corner – and almost hit the Williams. René Arnoux, lying second, was not so fortunate. The Frenchman's Ligier did not actually make contact with the Williams, but struck the wall instead. Arnoux then compounded his mistake by reversing from behind Piquet's car and then driving straight into the Arrows of Thierry Boutsen.

Piquet had crashed at 14.32. His car was not removed until 14.47. During that time, approximately 8 laps had been completed at racing speed. In 2007, such a potentially dangerous situation would have been avoided by use of the Safety Car, designed to slow the field while officials could work in safety on the track, particularly at a blind corner.

Now aware of the potential for chaos, Senna picked his way through the final corner and concentrated on maintaining what had become a 30-second lead for the remaining 22 laps. Senna's win placed him back at the head of the championship, deposing Prost who had won the previous race in Canada. Mansell was third in the title chase with Piquet fourth, the top four covered by 17 points.

This time, Senna did present himself at the press conference and made amends by patiently and courteously answering questions in the fascinating detail he could bring to such occasions when in the mood. Journalists of a certain age were to be reminded of Senna on Thursday, 14 June 2007.

9
At Home in Indiana

L ewis Hamilton sat before the United States motor sport media for the first time on Thursday, 14 June 2007. He almost did not make the appointment but, unlike Senna, Hamilton had a reasonable excuse. Following his win in Canada, the championship leader had little opportunity to celebrate. Sponsorship commitments in New York and Washington meant an early departure from Montreal on the Monday morning. With the United States Grand Prix following a week later, there was a limited amount of time to relax at a New York Yankees baseball game and enjoy the diminishing luxury of being able to walk the streets unnoticed. Hamilton's flight from Washington to Indianapolis the previous evening had been delayed because of bad weather and then cancelled altogether. An early morning departure on Thursday meant he had to go straight to the 11 a.m. press conference before he could even begin to take in the hallowed surroundings.

The Indianapolis Motor Speedway is as grand as it sounds. The 2.5-mile oval has been the central point of American auto racing since the running of the first Indianapolis 500-mile race in 1911. The 'Indy 500' may have diminished in stature due to political wrangling during the past ten years but nothing can detract from the awesome surroundings and the fact that this oval, built originally from 3.2 million bricks, has staged the richest motor race in the world.

Chequered Conflict

In 2000, it seemed perfectly logical that F1 and Indianapolis should unite, the speedway owners going out of their way to combine part of the famous oval with a specially constructed infield for F1 cars. The result may have been unimaginative in parts of the new section but use of one of the original banked corners brought a new dimension. Added to which were the ancient but magnificent facilities of the triple-tiered grandstand towering over the long main straight. The United States Grand Prix finally seemed to have found a decent home.

Hamilton had barely sat down in the interview room when questions started to flow about the latest outburst from his teammate. Alonso may have been unable to win on the track in Canada but he had been trying to make up psychological ground with the use of carefully crafted soundbites. The reigning world champion had suggested that since his team, McLaren, was British, then it was only natural that they might favour Hamilton. The quote, given to a Spanish radio station, had ruffled the carefully preened feathers of a management group that had gone to great lengths to ensure parity. McLaren's annoyance was exacerbated when some reporters then used Alonso's remarks to suggest the two drivers were at loggerheads and there was serious division within the team. This was news to Hamilton who, in any case, felt Alonso's remarks were a bit rich considering what had happened at Monaco. And Alonso had not yet finished. Returning to this subject as the teams gathered at Indianapolis, Alonso added another crafty twist:

There is no civil war. I never said anything against the team. In fact I said I had a competitive car, good enough to win my third consecutive title. What I said was that I was not totally comfortable. To be totally comfortable with the team there are things missing that I've talked to them about, and I think they are necessary to be comfortable, and things need to be done the way I think they need to be done.

It's things such as strategy, testing, sharing telemetry. But there are things that I thought would be different and it's not that way. That's the way I think and there's nothing more to it; it starts and ends there. The team have their reasons, their philosophy to prepare for qualifying and the race. I can agree with it or no. I prefer to keep my opinions to myself.

Alonso was doing precisely the opposite and, in the process, suggesting that the drivers did not share information, which went against the McLaren principle of having the engineers for both drivers discuss details gathered from, among other things, the telemetry that takes intricately detailed readings from each car when on the move. A member of the Renault team familiar with Alonso's methods said:

Fernando is a master at this sort of thing. He knows how to use the media, and that is exactly what he is doing. His method is 'silent assassin' and go quicker on the track. He is new at McLaren and his comments are a little attempt at reminding them that there's a double world champion in the team and not to forget it. If Lewis had a harder [more difficult] car, he would not be looking the equal of Fernando. Fernando is out of his comfort zone. He is doing something new with a new team. He's not in control and his team-mate is beating him. You could say that this is another test of his character.

While all of this was taking place, Hamilton smiled and got on with his job – but not without suggesting that perhaps Alonso had been surprised to find a novice team-mate capable of being fast enough to beat the Spaniard. 'I doubt he was expecting me to do as well as I am, but I don't know if that's why he is saying what he's saying,' said Hamilton. 'But definitely, coming into the team he is the two-time world champion and he's not really been challenged – well, I think he's had some challenges in the past – but he's not really had someone as close as me and [someone who is] as good a friend off the track probably, so it's a very difficult situation.'

Alonso responded by saying: 'I've had strong team-mates like [Jarno] Trulli in 2004, and I was behind him in the middle of the championship and I finished ahead of him in the end. And I've won a title ahead of [Kimi] Räikkönen and his McLaren, and another one ahead of Michael Schumacher. So I'm not easily surprised.'

Nonetheless, it would have taken a brave man to predict that Hamilton would be leading the championship by 8 points after just six of the season's seventeen races. Hamilton's meteoric progress had begun to attract worldwide attention, some of it just two states to the east of Indiana where the US Open was being played at Oakmont in Pennsylvania. Hamilton was delighted when told on the Thursday at Indianapolis that Tiger Woods had become one of his growing army of admirers.

'I didn't know that,' said Hamilton. 'I've never met him, I'm hopeless at golf but he's someone I admire greatly. That's put a smile on my face.' Not that he needed an excuse to beam broadly. Hamilton could let Alonso's comments go over his head because, as he said simply: 'I've got the best job in the world. I love it. I can't believe I'm here. I'm smiling every day.'

The smiles continued throughout the next three days, particularly Saturday and Sunday. As had happened in Canada, the McLarens had the measure of the Ferrari pair but it took Hamilton until the start of qualifying to unlock the final tenths of a second in the set-up of his car. There was nothing to chose between the two McLaren drivers. In the end, it was settled by Hamilton choosing to burn off more fuel in the final phase of qualifying, run lighter and claim pole even though it would mean that Alonso had more fuel in his tank at the start of the race and could therefore run longer. Hamilton thought it was worth the risk. He was also aware that Alonso would try to get the better of him during the very long run to the first corner.

True enough, the two cars were side-by-side, Hamilton on the inside as they approached the right-hander. Calm as you like, Hamilton began to edge to his left, the better to take the racing line into the first corner. Alonso, forced to back off, fell in behind his team-mate, the pair immediately pulling away from the Ferraris. When circumstances – fuel load and tyres – gave Alonso a marginally faster car in the middle phase of the race, he closed on the leading McLaren. A crucial moment came when Hamilton was held up slightly behind a back-marker as the leaders reached the very fast banked section leading on to the long main straight. Alonso saw his chance.

This was a severe test for any driver, never mind a novice in only his seventh Grand Prix. As everyone had come to expect, Hamilton under pressure showed a coolness that belied his twenty-two years. There was not a hint of a desperate defensive move or a locked brake as they ran side-by-side once again at 200 m.p.h. and braked for the 65 m.p.h. first corner. Alonso, well and truly dispatched, allowed his emotion to surface briefly at the end of that lap as he ran close to the pit wall beneath the McLaren management and shook his fist. Although never confirmed by the team, it is believed this was a reaction to the team refusing to concede to his request to have Hamilton let him through because he, Alonso, was faster. (When asked later why he had raised his hand when passing the pits, Alonso produced the unlikely explanation that he was blowing brake dust and accumulated bits of rubber from his sleeve.)

At that moment, Alonso was probably the only person at the speedway who disapproved of McLaren's policy of allowing their drivers to race each other (unlike Ferrari number two drivers who had been prevailed upon not to challenge Michael Schumacher during the previous ten years). Such a display of petulance can only have broadened Hamilton's smile as he crossed the line to score his second win within a week.

Chequered Conflict

Alonso's urge to show dissent manifested itself during post-race television interviews. McLaren insisted that their drivers don gleaming white imitation overalls designed to show sponsors' logos to good effect. It made a bizarre sight at Indianapolis when, after finishing first and second, the McLaren drivers seemed to be re-enacting a soap powder advert from the past with Hamilton having used the preferred product while Alonso's grubby race overalls appeared to have been washed in Brand X. Alonso was only too aware that Ron Dennis would be irritated beyond belief by a vision that was not in keeping with McLaren's squeaky clean image.

When the leading trio – Hamilton, Alonso and Massa – reached the media centre, Alonso was asked if he thought Hamilton's movements going into the first corner were fair.

'I don't know,' said Alonso. 'I think you need to see on TV. In the car, everything feels okay and we are fighting each other. You don't see many movements. So in the car I felt OK. I think on TV it will be maybe more easy to see.'

Almost before Alonso had finished, Hamilton gently interrupted. It was obvious that he wished to make his position clear.

'May I just say in the rules you're only allowed to make one move down the straight and going into the corner you're allowed to move back to your position or at least move back again to try and get yourself around the corner.'

It was immediately apparent that Hamilton was not willing to have innuendo colour what had been another very fine victory. Seven races run and Hamilton was leading the championship with 58 points. Alonso was 10 behind – a full race victory – with Massa on 39. Räikkönen, who had finished fourth, was next, with 32 points. After just 20 laps of this race, Räikkönen had fallen a massive 16 seconds behind Hamilton. Once again, few would have argued against Räikkönen's championship going the same way.

10
Brits at Home

The front-page headline on the race morning edition of *The Red Bulletin* said: 'They're Back! Is this the Red Revival?' The cover shot showed a deliberately blurred image of Massa's Ferrari hurrying on its way to pole position for the French Grand Prix at Magny-Cours. Hamilton may have missed out by just 0.07 seconds, but Räikkönen's third place underlined the expected comeback by the team from Maranello.

Anyone who thought the Italians would take the North American defeats lying down had been disabused by Ferrari's work since Indianapolis. A new front wing was the most obvious indication of many changes, big and small, to the Ferrari's aerodynamics. The underlying problem had been making the car and the tyres work in unison immediately for one quick lap; the Ferrari:Bridgestone package had been good in a race situation but not for the instant demand of a qualifying lap. Tests at Silverstone, and now qualifying in France, showed that the car had been improved, the tyre problem being eased at the start of the lap at Magny-Cours where a very long and fast corner helped put temperature into the rubber. And, of the two Ferrari drivers, Massa was clearly The Man.

The headline on that week's edition of *Autosport* focused on Räikkönen's struggle at Ferrari. A typically well-reasoned story by Steve Cooper talked of the Finn's recognition by both Ferrari and his previous employer, McLaren, as being the fastest man in

F1; quicker, even, than Michael Schumacher. But the suggestion was that Schumacher's presence in the Ferrari pit during much of the first half of the season, coupled with his friendship with Massa, indicated that Ferrari's momentum, subconsciously or otherwise, might be with the Brazilian. Not that Räikkönen would have been perturbed unduly by that. The so-called 'Ice Man' rarely seemed bothered by anything. And that, Cooper reasoned, might be part of the problem as Räikkönen failed to apply himself to the post-practice and -race technical debriefs in the manner demanded by such a super-competitive season.

This supported the more obvious shortcomings when Räikkönen appeared to be asleep at the start in Malaysia (where Hamilton stole third place) and wanting aggression during a lacklustre drive in Bahrain. And now that Ferrari were making a comeback, a small mistake by Räikkönen during his best qualifying lap at Magny-Cours provided further indication that Massa might be the better long-term bet.

Nonetheless, it had to be said that the Ferrari performance in France, for all its improvement, did not reflect either the effort put in by Hamilton or the difficulties experienced by McLaren. Alonso's qualifying had been cut short by gearbox trouble which relegated the reigning world champion to tenth on the grid, a development that neither assisted his mission to reduce Hamilton's 10-point lead in the championship nor helped remove his embattled feeling within the team.

After expressing the anticipated concern about the effect of Alonso's problems on the McLaren team as a whole, Hamilton could not avoid showing unease about the progress made by Ferrari. Whereas McLaren had gone to America expecting serious trouble from Ferrari but come away with two comparatively easy wins, it was clear that the British team had not anticipated such a dramatic improvement by their main rival in France. Massa was enjoying the moment as he celebrated his fourth pole position of the season. Beaming he said:

It's definitely looking like a good weekend for us. We began to turn things around during the test at Silverstone and we've found that the improvement is continuing here, so that's encouraging. I wouldn't say we are in front of our competitors but at least we are back fighting. The times are very close. I can feel that the car is more consistent and is behaving better. I'm really pleased with pole because I was unable to put a good lap together during free practice but, when it mattered during qualifying, I was able to do it.

Hamilton's weekend had got off to a bad start when the complex electronics on the McLaren had shut down the Mercedes engine because it was running below the expected temperature during unseasonably cold conditions on the Friday morning. Alonso, meanwhile, had been more off the track than on it as he continued to adjust his driving style to come to terms with the unique demands of the standard Bridgestone tyre.

More serious was the loss of valuable running time on Saturday morning when the failure of a brake sensor forced the removal of part of the front suspension on Alonso's car. Alonso managed 2 flying laps and completed just 4 more during qualifying before the gearbox broke and ended his chances of fighting for a place on the front row. Hamilton, meanwhile, had been having his own problems completing an error-free lap when it mattered most during the closing minute of qualifying:

You can't be perfect all the time. The car was really sweet for qualifying. I really feel it was good enough for pole but I lost time when I braked a little bit late for the corner at the end of the final straight. That cost me time but, even so, I'm very happy to be on front row. I know I've been on pole for the past two races but I'm not disappointed by this. Before the start of the season, I had never imagined I would be fighting for pole at this stage. I was not at the Silverstone test but the team were there and I could feel that the car is a bit more consistent. But fair play to Felipe; he did a great job. It was a good battle between us. When you are on the track, you are competing against each other even though we get on very well.

As if to prove it, Hamilton congratulated Massa with a genuine warmth that indicated the respect between the two. Hamilton knew he would have to deal with Räikkönen's Ferrari but his unspoken thought had to be making the most of Alonso's absence at the front and the possible constraints imposed by a team still desperate to give each driver equal treatment. McLaren must have felt helpless when, after a virtually trouble-free season thus far, both problems on Saturday afflicted the same car. Unfortunately for Ron Dennis, it belonged to the Spanish driver rather than the British one.

Alonso knew that his chances of scoring a decent result would be severely handicapped by starting from the middle of the grid. Sure enough, he spent most of the 70-lap race embroiled in battles with the likes of Heidfeld's BMW and the Renault of Giancarlo Fisichella. For the second time in three races, Alonso came home seventh. He was not happy about it, particularly as Hamilton had finished on the podium for the eighth race in succession.

He may not have won, but Hamilton realized that third place was as good as it was going to get. Räikkönen had got the jump on the McLaren at the start before running in tandem with his team-mate. By carrying more fuel and running later than Massa, Räikkönen was eventually able to take the lead and win for the first time since the opening round in Australia. He may have been the last of the four championship favourites but this was the start of a slow but very sure comeback. Time would show that *The Red Bulletin* had the wrong man on their cover.

Hamilton now led the championship by 14 points. His seemingly inexorable rise was reflected by the odds on two Betfair markets. Opening the season as a 37–1 outsider to take the drivers' title, Hamilton was trading as odds-on favourite at 4–6. Beyond the F1 scene, Hamilton was already being regarded as the most likely winner of the BBC Sports Personality of the Year, due to be held five months later. Having opened that market at 99–1, the betting on Hamilton had switched to 1–5. Jenson Button, the absolute British F1 hero after his first win the previous year but now struggling with a woefully uncompetitive Honda, was being quoted at 399–1 for the BBC prize.

The surge in interest at Button's expense became even more evident to Hamilton a few days later when he began preparations for the British Grand Prix. The test session at Silverstone had been attended by 20,000 people, an extraordinary number for a midweek event that was nothing more than endless laps as the teams went about the business of developing their cars. And Hamilton was not even present. That might have been a disappointment to many of the fans but the attendance figure was a sure sign of F1's return to prominence thanks largely to Hamilton's exploits.

The Englishman scarcely had time to call his own. A personal highlight had been a visit to the Daytona kart track at Milton Keynes to witness youngsters fighting out the final round of a championship. Hamilton was completely relaxed and in his element as he spoke to the miniature racers and gave advice on how to go about furthering their careers. They hung on every word and watched in awe as Hamilton left by helicopter for Silverstone and the start of more serious business.

Silverstone is a track of two distinct and disparate parts. There is a very quick section from the start line, through Copse, Maggots and Becketts and all the way round to Club corner, the drivers touching the brakes just once at Stowe corner at the top end of the circuit. Then the mood changes through Club and the Abbey chicane before a quick right-hander at Bridge and then a stuttering succession of slow corners through the final infield section.

Chequered Conflict

Following on from Magny-Cours, the Ferraris had the upper hand through the fast sections that made up the majority of the circuit, the McLarens enjoying a small advantage in the slow stuff at the end. In addition, Hamilton was struggling to make his car work to his usual standard of perfection. It was to his credit that he somehow found time in the fast section on his final qualifying lap to take pole. The crowd went wild. What they did not know was that Hamilton's car was running deliberately light, the better to give him a chance of being quickest. But that did not detract from one of the best qualifying laps ever seen at Silverstone as Hamilton dipped into his abundant well of natural ability and swept aside the Ferraris of Räikkönen and Massa, who were expected to occupy the front row. Hamilton said:

> That was very special. Obviously I'd hoped to be on pole but I have to admit it wasn't looking good during the first part of qualifying. I had been struggling to fine-tune the car. Experience is so critical at this circuit. You need to build up to the limit and it was all down to the last lap. I tried to take the first corner [Copse, approached at 180 m.p.h.] faster than ever before. I tried not to lift [his foot from the throttle] but didn't quite do it! Even so, I knew I had found a bit of time through there.
>
> Then the pressure is really on. You know you're on the way to a good lap but you also know that the slightest mistake and you've lost it. It was a phenomenal feeling to put that lap together. I was shouting into my helmet all the way through the slowing down lap – and it's a very long lap at Silverstone. I was hoarse at the end of it.

Hamilton added to the drama by being the last of the four favourites to cross the line at the end of the 3.2-mile lap. There was an element of good fortune thanks to Räikkönen having ruined his last lap by making an error and sliding wide at the final corner.

'I can't hide my disappointment,' said Räikkönen. 'I finished up on the grass and lost traction, which cost me too much time. But it's not worth spending too long thinking about it. What's done is done. We have a good pace over a long run and a lot will depend on the start and the strategy worked out by the team.'

Had he not run wide, the Ferrari driver would have been on pole, relegating Hamilton to the outside of the front row on the dirty side of the track, the same circumstances that had caused Hamilton to make a comparatively slow start in France. But now he was ideally placed to dictate the race, an important tactical consideration on a track where the Ferraris were potentially faster, certainly on the first two-thirds of the lap.

The 70,000 crowd – a record for practice at Silverstone – rising to pay their respects, had marked Hamilton's progress on his slowing down lap. None of this was lost on Alonso, who was running more fuel and had to accept second best within McLaren and third place on the grid. Alonso made no excuses. The Spaniard's hope lay with a different race strategy leap-frogging him ahead during the pit stop sequence. It looked like being his only hope, given Hamilton's outstanding form at home. Hamilton said:

I've been doing a lot of work for our sponsors and appearances and so on this week. But I feel quite relaxed this weekend. I like to make people happy when I'm out there. I get such a buzz and energy from the support. For sure there is pressure, but the most pressure comes from me. At other circuits, you see groups of support around the track but here, it's every grandstand. I really do appreciate the support and you definitely get a confidence boost from that. I keep pinching myself. It's still an experience that's difficult to get used to.

Chequered Conflict

If Hamilton seemed more preoccupied before the start it was because he knew he would have his work cut out. Yet all around him, the expectation was palpable. He had won twice already and, starting from pole, everything seemed possible. The reality would be different.

Hamilton would pay the price for running light during qualifying. He held the lead but stopped first, as expected. Both Räikkönen, who had been shadowing the McLaren and, at one point, tried to overtake, ran longer and moved ahead, as did Alonso. Hamilton, still struggling to make the car work, dropped back and was lucky to finish third. Had Massa not been forced to start from the pit lane after stalling on the grid, then he, too, would probably have been ahead and denied Hamilton his record run of podium finishes. At the halfway point in the season, Hamilton had 70 points, Alonso 58, Räikkönen 52, with Massa dropping to fourth, one point behind his team-mate.

It said much about Hamilton's perceived image and the expectation driven by his pole position that those on the outskirts of the sport should see anything less than victory as a disappointment. As Nigel Mansell would have said had he been present, nothing changes.

11

Mansell's Good Fortune

When Nigel Mansell arrived at Brands Hatch for the 1986 British Grand Prix, he was expected – no, he was required – to repeat his win of the previous weekend in France. That result had brought Mansell to within 1 point of the championship leader, Alain Prost. Emotion, which had been running high during the build-up to the British race, was turned up another notch when Frank Williams made a return to the paddock on the first day of practice and received a standing ovation as he was brought to the media centre for his first public appearance since the accident four months previously.

Williams, his voice barely audible, took no credit for the subsequent success of his team, preferring to pay tribute to the well-oiled operation he had put in place. It was appropriate, therefore, that the Williams-Honda team should go on to occupy the front row, the only change to a perfect script, from a British point of view, being the presence of Piquet on pole, rather than Mansell. The Brazilian, determined not to be cowed by his teammate's recent success, had produced a scintillating lap while, to be fair to Mansell, the Englishman had endured a catalogue of problems, most of which he was happy to share at length with anyone who would listen. Which meant the majority of a British media hanging on their hero's every word.

The 115,000 crowd – a record for Brands Hatch – was entertained on race morning by an air display that included Concorde and the massive Vulcan bomber. With jingoism stoked nicely, the fans knew much would depend on the start, history showing that the pole position man at Brands Hatch would be hampered by the track's steep camber at that point.

Sure enough, Mansell made the better start. Everything seemed to be going according to plan – at least for the first few seconds. As Mansell snatched second gear while forging into the lead, an explosion at the rear of the Williams announced the failure of a drive-shaft coupling. His race was over. But the news had barely reached the capacity crowd when the race took an even more dramatic turn.

Thierry Boutsen lost control on the uphill approach to the first corner, Paddock Bend. The Arrows went from right to left, hit the barrier and spun into the path of at least nine back-markers as they crested the rise. Cars went everywhere, one of them, the Ferrari of Stefan Johansson, swerving right and forcing the Ligier of Jacques Laffite to do the same. This was at the point where a tunnel to the paddock ran beneath the circuit. Johansson clipped the barrier surrounding the mouth of the tunnel but Laffite rammed the steelwork head-on. With cars not needing to undergo the challenging impact tests mandatory in 2007, the front of the Ligier folded up. Dr Jonathan Palmer, then a driver for Zakspeed and, later, to become the owner of Brands Hatch, had been caught in the accident. As Palmer sprinted to the aid of Laffite, the race was stopped. On seeing the Ligier's steering had been shoved into the driver, Palmer knew the news would not be good. It took thirty-five minutes to stabilize Laffite and free him from what was left of the cockpit. The Frenchman was flown to hospital in nearby Sidcup, where he was found to have injuries to his legs and pelvis. The popular Frenchman, a winner of six Grands Prix, knew that his F1 career was over because of an accident not of his making. As Kubica demonstrated so spectacularly in Montreal, had this happened in 2007, Laffite would have walked away.

The efficiency of the marshalling and rescue teams at Brands Hatch was in contrast to scenes a week before in France. Having already been censured for their inadequacies at the time of the fatal accident to de Angelis, the French organizers received a $20,000 fine for delaying the start of practice by leaving a mobile television crane locked and parked on the circuit. Worse was to follow on race day when a car caught fire at the entrance to the pit lane. It is true that matters were exacerbated by a disconnected fuel line continually pumping petrol on to a hot turbocharger thanks to the driver forgetting to switch off the electric pump before jumping out. The organizers could only be thankful that the driver had managed to vacate the cockpit rather than find himself trapped because the marshals' efforts to extinguish the flames would have been pure slapstick had the situation not been so serious. Then, as a final act in this comedy of errors, a giant fire tender when called to the scene travelled down the pit lane against the flow of incoming cars. The race was still in progress and there was no pit lane speed limit in 1986.

At Brands Hatch, the race was suspended for 80 minutes while the wreckage was cleared and the helicopter returned from Sidcup. The race would start afresh, which was good news for Mansell, the spare car having been prepared in readiness. Mansell had found that he did not like the back-up car (which had been set up for Piquet) after driving it briefly during practice and he made a circumspect getaway from the front row at the restart. But Mansell being Mansell, it did not take long before he was on the tail of the leader, Piquet.

With the vast majority of fans showing visible support for their home hero, perhaps it was not surprising that Piquet should miss a gear as the leaders accelerated out of a left-hand corner leading towards the back section of the circuit. Such an error – a chance for a pursuer to overtake – is not possible today thanks to semi-automatic gearboxes and the driver simply

Chequered Conflict

needing to flick a paddle on the steering wheel in order to change gear. In 1986, there were no sophisticated electronics to synchronize the throttle, clutch and gearbox. Piquet's coordination between his feet, brain and right hand had suffered a momentary glitch. In the couple of seconds necessary to sort it out, Mansell was already powering alongside and into the lead. By the time he returned to the main arena to complete the lap, the entire place had erupted.

Piquet did not give up. For the next 12 laps, the Williams pair left the rest of the field far behind. There was one pit stop remaining for fresh tyres. The Williams crew had Piquet away in 9.04 seconds; Mansell in 9.57 seconds. Had that happened in 2007 to Hamilton and Alonso, there would have been an inquiry (probably driven by the FIA) into why Alonso's stop had taken half a second longer than Hamilton's. But, in 1986, no one batted an eyelid. Both stops had been faultless: where was the problem?

Piquet's one last chance to overtake came as Mansell emerged from the pits, still in the lead. There had been a 2-lap gap between the two stops. Piquet's tyres were up to operating temperature whereas Mansell's were not, even though the recently introduced electric tyre blankets would help his cause. When Piquet tried to dive inside Mansell, he found the door slammed in his face. Piquet then attempted a slingshot move out of Paddock Bend a couple of laps later and the overtaking bid might have come off had a back-marker not been in the way. For the remaining 40 laps, the Williams pair went at it hammer and tongs, slashing the lap record as they went. Mansell had quickly discovered that the spare car did not have a drinks bottle on board (unthinkable by today's standards) and he was in a thoroughly dehydrated state as he crossed the line, 6 seconds ahead of Piquet.

Mansell said he had never driven so hard for 196 miles. In typically dramatic fashion, he needed a helping hand from officials (several of whom were on the winner's rostrum, a turnout which would be forbidden by the carefully orchestrated process today) as he tottered on the podium, a bemused Piquet and Prost looking on. Mansell had driven brilliantly to win four of the last five races, two in a week. He was now leading the championship on 47 points from Prost (who had finished second in France) on 43. Senna (retired from both races) had 36 and Piquet had 29. As Martin Brundle, who had been lapped three times in the fifth-place Tyrrell-Renault, observed: 'If Nigel can outdrive Piquet in equal cars, then he's ready to become world champion.' Few at Brands Hatch would have taken issue with that.

Unhappy with his lot, Piquet had begun to murmur to the Brazilian press that the Williams team, being British, appeared to be favouring Mansell, a complaint that would have a familiar resonance twenty-one years later. There may have been in-house rivalry and distrust in 1986 but that would have nothing on developments within McLaren that were about to tear both the team and F1 apart in 2007.

12

Technicians and Thieves

When Elio de Angelis was killed at Paul Ricard, Nigel Stepney felt the loss more than most. Stepney had first met the Italian when acting as a mechanic for Shadow, the small team with whom de Angelis had made his F1 debut in 1979. When de Angelis was snapped up by Lotus a year later, Stepney went with him but chose not to follow the driver to Brabham in 1986. Despite his friendship with de Angelis, Stepney could see that the prospects at Lotus were better, particularly as Ayrton Senna, an obvious star of the future, was part of the British team. When Senna moved to McLaren in 1988 and Lotus began a painful decline, Stepney went to Benetton to become chief mechanic. It was here that he met Michael Schumacher, the chemistry working successfully as Stepney played his part within a rapidly developing team.

F1 is a small, marginally incestuous world training people in highly specialist skills that, by and large, are useless anywhere else. Those that are good at their job find themselves much in demand. Stepney had built a reputation as a top organizer who understood the workings of F1 cars and, just as important, the people who built and serviced them. When John Barnard, the former McLaren designer who had broken dramatic new ground by introducing a carbon-fibre chassis to F1, moved from Benetton to Ferrari, he could see that the colourful and at times slightly hysterical Italian team was in desperate need of reorganization from the ground up.

Chequered Conflict

Stepney was the obvious choice, even though it would mean moving from his native England and integrating himself fully into the Italian – the Ferrari – way of life. Stepney embraced it fully. In addition, he knew things could only get better with the arrival at Ferrari of Jean Todt in 1993 and, three years later, Ross Brawn. Todt had been responsible for Peugeot's success in the World Rally Championship and Brawn had worked with Stepney as technical director at Benetton. The final ingredient was Michael Schumacher, with whom Brawn and Stepney had won two championships at Benetton.

It took time to lick everything into shape but, once on a roll, Schumacher and Ferrari won five world titles. Stepney was credited with an important part in all of this as he moved from chief mechanic to take charge of the internal organization of the race team and become largely responsible for making the cars reliable. It was a perfect partnership but the day had to come when the dream team would begin to break up.

When Schumacher retired at the end of 2006 and Brawn took a sabbatical, the restructuring of Ferrari's technical department did not meet Stepney's approval. While not expecting to assume Brawn's role, Stepney was not impressed when Ferrari gave that title to someone who had previously been in charge of human resources and, to the outside world, appeared to know little about the necessary technicalities. Ferrari were perfectly happy with their choice but relations between Stepney and his team were about to go into steep decline.

At the beginning of 2007, word began to circulate that the reorganization within Ferrari was causing a few problems. On 1 February, Steve Cooper of *Autosport* tried to make contact with Stepney through the Ferrari press office. Cooper was not surprised when the request was denied: most top teams are highly sensitive about their employees speaking to the media, and Ferrari is no exception. However, Cooper was amazed when, on the off-chance, he called the Ferrari switchboard, asked for

Stepney – and was put straight through. Discussion had not been under way for long when, unprompted, Stepney rolled a smoking bomb down the line.

'I am looking at spending a year away from Ferrari,' said Stepney. 'I'm not currently happy with the situation within the team – I really want to move forward with my career and that's something that's not happening right now. Ideally, I'd like to move into a new environment here at Ferrari – but if an opportunity arose with another team, I would definitely consider it.'

When the story was published, Ferrari were not amused. Stepney had another year to run on his contract – reputed to be worth more than £500,000 per annum – and the team were now determined to hold him to it. It was decreed that Stepney would be made head of Team Performance Development and would no longer travel to the races.

It was with some surprise that I bumped into Stepney in the departure lounge of Gatwick Airport on Thursday, 10 May. We had first met in 1982 when, as a mechanic with the Lotus team, Stepney had looked on with a wry smile as Nigel Mansell and I engaged in a heated discussion over something I had written criticizing an early performance by the English driver. Stepney, who had a permanent twinkle in his eye, appeared to enjoy, at the very least, witnessing confrontation, if not taking part in it. At the time, Stepney was well known for encouraging his mechanic colleagues to get up to no good but he had since mellowed with age and the arrival of well-earned responsibility.

Our relationship was typical of F1. Even though you are working within the same enclosed environment at the racetrack, you might not see someone for quite some time and then find yourselves sitting beside each other on a flight to a race or, occasionally, be sharing the same hotel and a late-night beer. I knew Stepney from our long-time association and we were more business acquaintances rather than bosom-buddies. Nonetheless, I had always enjoyed having chats on the understanding that if he said something was off the record, it would remain that way. As we enjoyed a drink in the British Airways lounge, it was clear from his collar and tie that this had probably been more than a social visit to his home country. Stepney did not reveal the exact nature of his trip but it was clear that he had been talking to a F1 team (later to be revealed as Honda) about prospective employment. Having generally discussed the F1 season thus far, we parted, Stepney boarding a plane to Italy while I flew to Barcelona. At no point had we touched on his problems with Ferrari. I knew he was unhappy and looking for work. Beyond that, I did not think it was hugely important. How wrong could I be?

What had so far been a domestic issue within Ferrari became more serious when, a few weeks later, the Modena district attorney opened a criminal investigation following a formal complaint by Ferrari over Stepney's conduct. While the precise details were not revealed, Italian newspapers were soon carrying stories connecting Stepney with sabotage. It was alleged that powder had been found in the fuel tank of a car prior to the Monaco Grand Prix on 27 May. Stepney denied allegations that, to most people involved in F1, seemed highly unlikely. First, there was no reason to think Stepney would do something as foolish and dangerous. Second, in the unlikely event he had done so, Stepney's intricate knowledge of a sophisticated Grand Prix car is such that, if he had sabotage in mind, something more devious than powder (believed to be washing detergent) in a fuel tank would have been employed. At 14.24 on 3 July, I sent Stepney a text message expressing surprise over the powder story and saying I realized he could not say much but, if he wanted to talk, I would be happy to hear and perhaps print his point of view. There was not an immediate response.

More likely, however, was Stepney's earlier involvement in the exposure of Ferrari having won the first race of the season with a car that was bending the rules. All of that was about to come to light in an extraordinary development during the days leading to the British Grand Prix, the start of a sequence of events that would threaten to tear the sport apart.

There was little surprise on Tuesday, 3 July, when Ferrari announced that Stepney had been dismissed. But there was disbelief later that day when McLaren issued the following statement:

McLaren became aware on 3 July that a senior member of its technical organization was the subject of a Ferrari investigation regarding the receipt of technical information.

The team has learnt that this individual had personally received a package of technical information from a Ferrari employee at the end of April.

Whilst McLaren has no involvement in the matter and condemns such actions, we will fully cooperate with any investigation.

The individual has, in the meanwhile, been suspended by the company pending a full and proper investigation of the matter.

No further comment will be made.

There might have been no further official comment from McLaren but the F1 world, a network of gossip at the best of times, went into overdrive. This was an extraordinary piece of news that had come out of the blue. Stepney was fingered immediately as the Ferrari employee and it did not take long for the leading McLaren suspect to emerge.

Mike Coughlan was McLaren's chief designer. The title is deceiving since it imbues the sense of one man having complete control of the shape of the McLaren F1 car. In fact, Coughlan was overseeing the general design concept while assimilating information from various specialist departments such as aerodynamics, chassis design and construction, electronics, engine manufacture and its installation in the car. Ron Dennis had made much of a so-called matrix management system that was horizontal rather than pyramidal in form, thus allowing openness and understanding between every section of the company. It was a structure that was about to be questioned and ridiculed in public, never mind within the company itself.

A talented 48-year-old, Coughlan had learned his trade with various teams, among them Lotus and Benetton (since renamed Renault), where he had worked with Stepney. Coughlan later worked with Barnard when the designer was a consultant to Ferrari, thus further strengthening the association with Stepney. While Stepney's disaffection with Ferrari had become obvious, there seemed no reason why Coughlan should feel the same about McLaren, with whom he had worked since 2002 and held a responsible and handsomely remunerated post.

As the teams gathered at Silverstone on Thursday, 5 July, the close confines of the paddock and the warren of motor homes accelerated the rumour process. Hard fact emerged that evening when Ferrari issued a statement:

> Ferrari announces it has recently presented a case against Nigel Stepney and an engineer from the Vodafone McLaren Mercedes team with the Modena Tribunal, concerning the theft of technical information.
>
> Furthermore, legal action has been instigated in England and a search warrant has been issued concerning the engineer. This produced a positive outcome.
>
> Ferrari reserves the right to consider all implications, be they criminal, civil or of any other nature, according to the applicable laws.

Investigators (not the police) acting on behalf of Ferrari had visited Coughlan's home at East Lightwater in Surrey. They had found a number of CDs, the production of which had actually been more important to this case than the information held within them. It would later transpire that Coughlan had received a 780-page manual on how Ferrari would operate in 2007. This contained a wealth of technical detail, from wind tunnel data to reports on test sessions, drawings of the 2007 Ferrari and a break-down of budgets and the team's innermost working practices. Given the bulky nature of a document that weighed 3.5 kilos (8 lbs), Coughlan decided to have the information transferred to disks, a move which would also facilitate the easy transfer of information from one computer to another. Coughlan's wife, Trudy, a former receptionist with the Tyrrell F1 team, took the manual to a company in Walton-on-Thames specializing in the transfer of paper documents to disks. This would be Mike Coughlan's downfall.

The manager of the company, realizing the sensitive nature of the material, telephoned the Ferrari headquarters in Maranello. Once through to Todt, and given the information to hand, it did not take long to convince the Ferrari chief executive officer that something was seriously amiss. Todt immediately contacted his lawyers in London, who then spoke to the company in Walton-on-Thames. From there it was a short journey in time for the lawyers to apply to the High Court in London for a Search Order and a visit to the Coughlan home. There, a massive can of worms was about to be opened. Without the call from the copy company, none of this would have come to light.

There were more questions than answers as the details began to emerge at Silverstone. This race coincided with the opening of McLaren's latest travelling headquarters; very different from the American-style motor homes the F1 teams had considered a luxury in 1986. McLaren had always been among the pacesetters when it came to expanding the motor homes into something bigger and better than their rivals could either manage or afford – assuming they were that bothered in the first place. McLaren, along with the British American Racing team, had set a trend a few years before by bringing structures that could be used to connect two mobile units. Now, McLaren had gone one further by introducing their so-called Brand Centre, a purpose-built three-storey, smoked-glass structure that took forty-eight hours to erect and dismantle and twelve trucks to carry the pieces from race to race in Europe, never mind the cranes needed to lift the heavier panels into place on site. It was Dennis's misfortune – the start of many such calamities in the coming months – that the official opening of the Brand Centre should come twenty-four hours after what was rapidly becoming known as 'spygate' had blown up in his face. As the media gathered, ostensibly to admire the latest in F1 facilities, the only questions were about espionage rather than architecture. It was an emotional moment for Dennis, but for all the wrong reasons. Dennis took a lengthy pause, composed himself and then said:

> I live and breathe this team. And there is no way anything incorrect would ever happen in our team. It has been a difficult two or three days, especially for me. My personal integrity is very important to me and my company's integrity is even more important to me. The press releases we have put out really say everything.
>
> We are in a process. We are working closely with the FIA and closely with Ferrari. This matter does not involve our company. Of course, that is not the way understandably everybody sees it at the moment. Some of you [the media] have been very supportive of McLaren, I think some of you have been a little harsh on McLaren. But I understand depending which country you are in, and depending on the information you have available to you, you are going to form opinions.
>
> I am absolutely confident that with the passing of time, and it is a little difficult to put any timing on it, you will see and the world will understand that McLaren's position is one that is reflective of our statements. We have never to my

knowledge, and certainly over the past few months over this period, ever used other people's intellectual property. It is not on our car. I am sure the FIA will confirm that either now or in the future, and that is the key message.

We are both ourselves, the FIA and Ferrari, going through a very careful process. And I have a complete confidence in the outcome. We are [also] completely focused on this week's Grand Prix, an important Grand Prix for us.

Glasses were raised to the future of the Brand Centre and success in racing rather than politics. The team's wine had come from New Zealand and an acclaimed producer known as Spy Valley. Under the circumstances, it was an unfortunate choice.

13
Spilling into Print

No sooner had the engines died down after the British Grand Prix than the rumour machine could be heard rumbling back to life. There was plenty to discuss, not least a statement in three morning newspapers by Nigel Stepney, saying that he was innocent of all charges.

The *Sunday Times*, *Independent on Sunday* and my newspaper the *Observer*, had carried the story. On the Friday evening, before leaving the track, Jane Nottage, the motor sport correspondent for the *Sunday Times* and a good friend of Stepney, had told me that he wanted to set the record straight by speaking to Jane, David Tremayne, the correspondent for the *Independent* and myself. We were to meet at the track at 8 a.m. on Saturday morning, before the media centre became busy, and speak to Stepney by phone. Stepney had gone to ground and it has to be confessed that there was a frisson of excitement in knowing we were about to speak to the one man whom many people in the paddock wished to interview – for various reasons.

Jane made the call and, after a brief word to Nigel from David and me, Jane spoke to Stepney for the remainder of the twenty-minute conversation. Jane asked the questions and repeated Stepney's answers to serve the dual purpose of allowing Nigel to hear his replies as Jane understood them and for Tremayne and me to record the words in writing.

Chequered Conflict

Stepney explained that he had been on holiday with his girl-friend, Ash, and their 1-year-old daughter, Sabine, when the news broke of the discovery of Ferrari Documents in Coughlan's home. Stepney said that harassment by unknown individuals had reached such an extent since his return that he had been forced to flee Italy.

'There have been high-speed car chases,' said Stepney. 'We've been followed by more than one car, with Italian plates, and when we cornered one of them last Thursday evening the men in it refused to speak. I don't believe they were journalists. Ash has been stalked at the house. There was tracking gear on my car. Someone was going to get hurt. I'd no option but to get out of Italy.'

Referring to his unhappiness at Ferrari, Stepney said: 'The first sign of a potential problem came in September last year [2006] when Ross Brawn said he would be taking a sabbatical and the technical management structure would be changing.'

Discussions with Todt led to Stepney taking responsibility for the race and the test teams. Stepney said:

I wanted to report to Aldo Costa, the head of chassis design. He was the right person to respond to. I didn't want to respond to Mario Almondo, the new technical director.

By mid-February, the relationship had started to break down. I couldn't work with them. I missed the one-to-one relationship with Ross. He knew exactly what I could do; I always had 100 per cent support from Ross. Now I had four or five people to report to. It was very frustrating.

I told Jean Todt I didn't want to travel any more. I wanted to sit back and consider the future. Ferrari took that badly. My role became head of performance development based at the factory. I began to feel like I was some sort of traitor, just because I no longer wanted to travel.

At that stage, I wasn't looking anywhere else. But

whenever I discussed anything with people in the factory in the course of doing my job, it got fed back to senior management. People became scared to talk to me. I was put in a position where it was difficult to do my job. By the end of March the situation was unbearable. I started to look at other teams, and approached Nick Fry [CEO of the Honda F1 team].

I met up with Mike [Coughlan] at the end of April [the 28th, in Port Ginesta in Spain]. I'd had one meeting with Nick and didn't want to go into a second one alone. At first, Mike wasn't looking at a move, although he was unhappy with the McLaren management. Then three or four people at Ferrari indicated to me, after reading stories of my approach to Honda, that they would be interested in joining a technical group to go to another team. They wanted to follow us to go into a structure in which they felt comfortable.

I categorically deny that any technical information passed between Mike and I during that meeting, or at any time. We mainly discussed the sort of infrastructure and tools we would need to get the job done in another team. I saw the future as helping to put such a structure into place at Honda.

This theory tallied with what I had heard from Stepney during our chance encounter at Gatwick Airport on 10 May. Stepney explained that the key to success in F1 is bringing a cohesive working unit to a struggling team rather than one person accepting a high-ranking role and attempting to merge with an existing operation and its inherent faults. During the phone call at Silverstone Stepney said:

You don't just take one team's structure and bang it into another team. These things have to evolve, but Mike and I agreed to pool our expertise and talked about what we could bring to a team. Then we met Nick Fry together on 1 June at Heathrow.

On 17 May, when there were legal moves against me by Ferrari, people were taken from the factory to the Carabinieri headquarters to be interviewed, but no charges were made against anyone. My house in Serramazzoni has been raided twice.

After the thing with the Carabinieri, I called Jean Todt to say I was going on holiday to the Philippines (I'd filled in the relevant form but it was on my desk and I hadn't handed it in), and wouldn't be coming back until this was all sorted out. We haven't spoken since.

Stepney had been unaware of the development with Coughlan until contacted by a British journalist that week and asked about the discovery of Ferrari Documents and the connection between the two former workmates. Stepney said:

I admit it looks blatantly obvious. But something is happening inside Ferrari. I was accused by Mario Almondo of taking some drawings. I had them in my possession legitimately because I needed them for work on the simulator, but it was reported by to him by the drawing office that I had them. I got the papers and threw them on Almondo's desk. The next day they were back on mine!

I categorically deny that I copied them, or that I sent them to Mike Coughlan. I knew I was being watched all the time at the factory, that everything I did or said was being reported back, and that people knew whenever I accessed files on the computer. I have no idea how anything came into Mike's possession. I don't even know for sure that he has had documents. Do you know for sure? Categorically, he didn't get them from me. If he has some, then they came from another source.

I would be a bit stupid to go anywhere if I had such material, wouldn't I? I put a lot of the systems and working practices in place at Ferrari, relating to the operations of the test and race teams and the preparation of the cars, information I am told was supposed to be in the documents. I had worked on them with Ross and Aldo Costa. So if I already had all that material in my head, why would I need it all again?

I have nothing to hide; I might as well have left the keys to my house with the caretaker so anyone from Ferrari could go in. Ferrari is terrified that what I have in my mind is valuable.

I'm just a bit confused. I was never a yes man, and as soon as I went against the system at Ferrari, I got squeezed. Ferrari is unique in Italy, it's a religion. If you go against it, it's like going against the Vatican. I'm anxious, naturally, but I haven't done anything wrong and I believe in the legal system in Italy.

I duly filed this bombshell with the *Observer*. The paper ran a headline on the front page of the sports section as well as giving an entire page inside to Stepney over and above the eight-page pull-out devoted to the British Grand Prix. I walked into the Silverstone paddock on Sunday morning, aware that this would cause a furore within Ferrari. A reaction was not long in coming.

Luca Colajanni's business card carries the title 'Gestione Sportiva. Responsabile Stampa' beneath the Ferrari prancing horse emblem. A more dedicated press officer is difficult to find in the F1 paddock, Colajanni seeing his red uniform as a badge of honour. His face probably matched the colour of his beloved cars when he picked up the selection of British Sunday newspapers and caught sight of the *Observer*. By 11 a.m., I had been asked to go to his office within the Ferrari hospitality area. Spread before him was *Observer* Sport, the front of which carried the headline

Chequered Conflict

'Ferrari "spy" flees Italy in fear' and, beneath it, a 500-word sum-mary by Oliver Owen, the paper's deputy sports editor and motor sport fan. Inside, on page eight, was the sorry tale in full.

To say Colajanni was upset would be an understatement. This was difficult for both of us. I liked and respected Colajanni and the feeling was probably mutual because he looked hurt more than anything else. We both had our jobs to do. Here was arguably the best story of the weekend in the whole of sport, never mind F1, and yet the unspoken impression seemed to be that I was a member of the F1 'family' and should not have run such a scurrilous tale. He continually stabbed his finger at the page, saying 'Lies! All lies!'

Perhaps it was indeed a scandalous story but Stepney's words had, at that stage, to be taken at face value. We had asked on three separate occasions if he had supplied Coughlan with the documents and three times Stepney has been emphatic in his denial. On the Saturday, Jane Nottage had asked to speak to Jean Todt for a reaction to comments we had from Stepney, but the opportunity had been denied. I told Colajanni that Ferrari had the right of reply and the *Observer* would devote as much space as necessary the following week. He remained very upset. I understood that. If I had been in his position, I would have felt exactly the same. We parted uneasily, but with a handshake. If I thought that was bad, much worse was to come as this story took on a terrible life of its own.

On the Thursday of the following week, the FIA issued a statement.

Representatives of Vodafone McLaren Mercedes have been requested to appear before an extraordinary meeting of the FIA World Motor Sport Council in Paris on Thursday, July 26, 2007.

The team representatives have been called to answer a charge that between March and July 2007, in breach of

Article 151c of the International Sporting Code, Vodafone McLaren Mercedes had unauthorized possession of documents and confidential information belonging to Scuderia Ferrari Marlboro, including information that could be used to design, engineer, build, check, test, develop and/or run a 2007 Ferrari Formula One car.

Coughlan and his wife had agreed to sign a sworn affidavit detailing everything they knew in return for Ferrari ceasing High Court proceedings against them. The affidavit had become the most valuable and sought-after document in motor sport. In it lay the answers for many questions, not the least being whether McLaren-Mercedes were about to be thrown out of the world championship, thus wrecking Hamilton's dream debut at a stroke. The affidavit might also lead to the discovery of how much – if any – of the information had been used by McLaren, as well as helping Ferrari uncover the source of the leak within their headquarters.

For the moment, however, greater interest surrounded McLaren's connection with what appeared to be an act of gross stupidity by their senior designer. That seemingly unwitting involvement by McLaren took a more serious turn when the FIA issued the press release and called the team to the WMSC meeting on 26 July. If, as suspected, the FIA had seen Coughlan's affidavit, then it was enough to raise questions and prompt the charge that McLaren was in unauthorized possession of confidential information that could have been used to further their cause in the 2007 championship.

Ron Dennis continued to state that their present car, the McLaren MP4/22, had not been influenced by Ferrari in either its manufacture or its running. Dennis was seen as having many faults, but deceit and guile were not among them. While that opinion would be subject to review a few weeks later, for the time being and unfortunately for Dennis, personal probity would not be enough if one of his employees had acted unlawfully. It would be even worse if, as suspected, Jonathan Neale, McLaren's managing director, had knowledge of Coughlan's possession of the Ferrari Documents. The question was: how long did he know? Dennis had made mention of Coughlan having the information at the end of April: the FIA statement mentioned March, thus opening the timespan of possible knowledge and making it more difficult for McLaren to prove that none of it had been used for either the team's benefit or, just as significant, as a weapon against Ferrari.

In the light of that information, wider issues were coming under consideration. It suddenly seemed an interesting coincidence that McLaren should have drawn the FIA's attention to the fact that Ferrari were running a flexible floor on their cars in Melbourne in mid-March, thus revisiting the question: how did McLaren know about the exploitation of the loophole?

If McLaren were found to have made use of the detailed workings of their main rival, then the FIA could chose from a number of penalties, ranging from a fine to exclusion from one or two future races, to the ultimate punishment of removal from the 2007 world championship. Hamilton and Alonso could automatically be kicked out of the drivers' championship even though they were entirely innocent.

Precedents include the banning of the Tyrrell team for a technical infringement in 1984, Martin Brundle being stripped of a brilliant second-place finish in the Detroit Grand Prix. More recently, Jenson Button and Honda were excluded from the 2005 San Marino Grand Prix and banned from the next two races – including the Monaco showpiece – when the car was found to have a hidden fuel tank.

Much would depend on the FIA's interpretation of Article 151c of their International Sporting Code. It prohibits 'any fraudulent conduct or any act prejudicial to the interests of any competition or to the interests of motor sport generally'. Before then, however, F1 would return to its core business. The political turmoil may have been deadly serious but, for Lewis Hamilton, motor racing would become, for a few alarming moments, a matter of life and death.

14

Win Some,
Lose Some

ewis Hamilton had about five seconds in which to realize his remarkable good fortune was coming to a painfully abrupt end. That was the time it took during qualifying at the European Grand Prix for a front wheel on his McLaren-Mercedes to work loose and send the Englishman into a tyre barrier at more than 120 m.p.h.

Hamilton had just left the pits after a tyre change prior to what should have been his penultimate qualifying lap. The air-gun used to tighten the right-front wheel had given a wrong reading. The nut, which appeared secure, had not been tightened sufficiently and began to work loose halfway round the lap at the point where Hamilton was reaching 155 m.p.h. on the approach to a left-hand curve. The plan was to take the corner flat out.

The tyre made contact with the sharp edge of a carbon-fibre body part and immediately deflated, giving Hamilton very little steering and reduced braking as he attempted to turn into the corner. The McLaren went straight on, launched itself off a kerb and barely touched a gravel run-off area before coming to a sudden stop, nose-first, in a tyre barrier. It was a massive impact.

Hamilton immediately felt pain. He felt sure he had broken a leg and fractured a rib, at the very least. The front of the car was intact but Hamilton's body language, as he struggled from the cockpit and tried but failed to stand on his right leg, suggested that all was not well with the driver.

Chequered Conflict

Hamilton was stretchered to a waiting support vehicle and taken to the track's medical centre, where it was established that no bones had been broken. When he was flown by helicopter from the Nürburgring to a local hospital for further observation, it was discovered that the damage was confined to the top muscles of his chest and a ruptured ligament between his ribs. Hamilton, who knew nothing about the background to the McLaren–Ferrari scandal, was even less inclined to care as he worried about his participation in this race and the effect his absence might have on the championship. After a rigorous examination, the doctors declared him fit to take part, a conclusion that was confirmed on race morning during an assessment by the FIA medical delegate, Dr Gary Hartstein. Hamilton may have been tenth on the grid, but at least he was racing.

Qualifying had been halted for more than 15 minutes while Hamilton was attended to and his wrecked car removed. The delay, with just 5 minutes of running time remaining, had proved a test of temperament as the nine drivers in the final shoot-out waited for the opportunity to squeeze in just one quick lap. Typically for the driver known as 'Ice Man', Räikkönen had set the fastest time, his second pole position of the season following on the heels of the victories in France and Great Britain.

'The waiting was difficult,' admitted Räikkönen. 'You just have to be patient. There was only one chance and my lap was good enough for pole. It's been difficult to do this [since his previous pole at the first race in Australia] but I've done it at a time when there is now just one McLaren to worry about.'

Räikkönen was referring to Hamilton's removal from the leading runners and Alonso's position alongside the Ferrari on the front row. Alonso considered himself lucky to be there after running wide during his fastest lap. Referring to Hamilton's crash he said:

It's never easy – and even worse when something happens to one of your cars. You have to focus on your job but, during those moments, it's not nice to sit in your car and wait. It's easy to lose concentration and momentum because you have only one lap left. I lost [control of] the car in turn 5 [a 110 m.p.h. left-hand corner] and I was trying to control it for 50 or 60 metres. I had been faster [than Räikkönen] until that point but, obviously, I knew I had lost pole position. I thought the best I could do was finish the lap as neatly as possible and maybe qualify fifth or sixth. I was very surprised to find myself second.

Alonso was assisted by Felipe Massa being affected even more than the Spaniard by the stoppage.

'Everything had been very good during the first two parts of qualifying,' said Massa. 'But when we got to the final third, I seemed to lose momentum after the delay. I couldn't manage the perfect lap and had to take third. But at least we know that the car is quick.'

The McLaren team faced the difficulty of preparing the spare chassis for Hamilton. The days had since passed when mechanics would take as long as required to rebuild and prepare the cars for the race. In a case such as this, where a car had been badly damaged, the team would have knuckled down to an 'all-nighter', which was exactly what it said, the mechanics falling into bed just before dawn for a brief rest – if they were lucky.

All of that had changed with the introduction of the 'parc fermé' rule at the beginning of the 2003 season. This called for the teams to deliver their cars to a secure area at the end of Saturday afternoon. They would be returned on race morning, but work on the cars would be seriously limited. The following year, in a further bid to reduce costs, drivers would be required to use the same engine throughout the race weekend. If the engine needed to be changed, the driver would suffer a ten-place penalty on the grid. In 2007, the life of the engine had to stretch through two races. McLaren therefore faced a dilemma when reviewing the situation with Hamilton's car. The crashed MP4/22 was beyond immediate repair, necessitating the use of the spare car for the race. But if the team could manage to switch the engine from the crashed car to the spare then, clearly, Hamilton would not suffer a grid penalty for using to a fresh engine (the one already in the spare car).

While waiting for the wrecked car to emerge from parc fermé at 08.30 on race morning, the team removed the engine from the spare chassis in readiness to receive the Mercedes V8 and transmission from the crashed car. The hope was that the engine had not suffered unseen damage during the impact. All of the telemetry readings, plus a rigorous examination of the engine's oil by the ExxonMobil technician, Dr Tony Harlow, indicated that everything appeared to be in order. But no one could be 100 per cent sure.

It seemed likely that Hamilton would finish the race in the top eight but, as things would work out, his starting position would seriously compromise his chances of scoring a championship point, never mind continuing his remarkable run of nine podium finishes in his first nine races. The notoriously fickle Nürburgring weather was about to stand this race and Hamilton's season on its head.

Most teams were agreed that rain was due to arrive within three minutes of the start but none was prepared to take the risk of running a wet-weather tyre for as long as the track remained dry. The only gamblers were the Spyker team who felt they had nothing to lose with both cars starting from the back of the grid. Spyker split their options, leaving Adrian Sutil on dry tyres but bringing in debutant Markus Winkelhock (replacing Christijan Albers, who had been sacked) for wet-weather tyres at the end of the parade lap. It was to be a clever move.

No sooner had the field completed the first lap of racing than the rain arrived, suddenly and violently. It was so bad that, even after stopping at the pits for wet-weather tyres, several drivers were mere passengers as their cars skated off the track on the downhill approach to the first corner. Among them was Hamilton, who had had a dramatic race thus far.

Starting from tenth, the McLaren was into fourth place at the exit of the first corner. Then it all went wrong as the BMW drivers collided and a spinning Heidfeld caught Hamilton's left-rear tyre and punctured it. This appeared to be providential because, by the time Hamilton had limped into the pits, it was clear that wet-weather tyres were the thing to have. But not even Hamilton's burgeoning skill could save the car as he left the pits to find that a river of water had appeared at the first corner. In this seesaw weekend of emotion for the young man, Hamilton somehow managed to keep the engine running despite being embedded in the gravel run-off area. It made a remarkable sight as a crane manoeuvred into position, picked up the McLaren, dropped it on the track and Hamilton motored gently away. It would have been no surprise to see him wave the crane driver goodbye, such was this bizarre scene a reminder of gentler, less frantic times. By now, the race had been red-flagged, the only sensible option given the terrible conditions.

Just as quickly, the track began to dry and the drivers prepared for the restart on dry-weather tyres. At the head of the field was none other than Winkelhock thanks to Spyker's smart move. A lead of 30 seconds – and this despite a second stop to change from wet-weather tyres to the so-called extreme wet or monsoon tyre – had vanished with the red flag and it was clear the leading runners, potentially 3 seconds a lap faster than the orange and grey Spyker, would soon dismiss the young German on this extraordinary debut. Sure enough, Massa, Alonso and Räikkönen got by and set off to dispute a race that was certain to go the way of one of these three.

The choice narrowed to two when Räikkönen's appalling luck at the Nürburgring – he had twice lost the lead when racing for McLaren – struck again with hydraulics failure. It was a serious blow because the Finn had looked strong and was poised to add to the maximum points collected in France and Britain. Meanwhile, Massa appeared to be able to keep Alonso at arm's length while Hamilton, now out of sequence on the pit stops, fought hard to get into the top ten, having taken the restart in seventeenth place. Alonso later admitted there was little he could do about the Ferrari but he was happy to accept the 8 points for second place. Then the dice rolled once more.

With 10 laps remaining, the rain reappeared, not so heavy this time but bad enough to prompt a return to wet-weather tyres. Sniffing his third win of the season, Alonso went for it. He hunted down Massa, the Ferrari driver struggling with vibration from his Bridgestones. Alonso tried everything and eventually made his presence felt around the outside of the 120 m.p.h. left-hander at turn 5 – the very place where his mistake during qualifying had cost him pole position. The two cars banged wheels, inflicting damage to the side-pod of the McLaren – but Alonso emerged in front. Meanwhile, Hamilton had rapidly caught the eighth place Renault of Kovalainen but the Finn hung on to take a point at the end of one of his best races of the season.

Alonso, on the one hand, was the happiest man at the Nürburgring, having scored 10 points on a day when Hamilton, for the first time, had failed to finish on the podium and scored no points at all. On the other hand, Alonso was not pleased with Massa and the two had a heated exchange while preparing to go on to the podium. According to a Spanish journalist listening in on the conversation, the narrative went like this:

Alonso: You did it on purpose.
Massa: Go away! Fuck you. You win and that's your
    behaviour? You still have a lot to learn!
Alonso: The one who still has a lot to learn is you. Three
    laps and you almost finish fifth. Look how good a
    driver you are.

Massa: Yes, I did it on purpose, like in Barcelona. [A barbed
reference to Alonso running wide while attempting
to take the lead from Massa at the first corner in
Spain.]

By the time the press conference had been called not long after,
Alonso had calmed down enough to apologize. But it was yet
another element to an increasingly overwrought season as
Alonso closed to within 2 points of, arguably, his biggest rival:
Lewis Hamilton.

This had been part of a continuing and steep learning curve
for the Englishman. He took it in good heart, knowing he was
fortunate not to have been seriously hurt the previous day.
Indeed, his only major concern after the race was wondering
what exactly to do with himself since, on the previous nine occasions, he had followed all the procedures connected with going
straight to the podium. Now, having climbed from his car, he
had to make his own way to the paddock and the waiting posse
of British press.

The media were to assemble once more on 26 July when the
World Motor Sport Council hearing in Paris examined the so-
called Ferrari–McLaren spygate affair. Once the result had been
made known, it was difficult to tell whether Ferrari's outrage
was generated by McLaren being exonerated or the fact the
British team had snatched a certain victory from Ferrari a few
days before. Neither result went down well in Italy although,
judging by Ferrari's virulent accusation that justice had not been
done in the former, results on the racetrack had been marginal-
ized by proceedings in the courtroom. The majority verdict
of the World Council was that McLaren had indeed been in
possession of information belonging to another team, but there
was no proof that this had been employed by McLaren for their
own ends.

Ferrari's reaction was both rapid and rancorous, the Italian team accusing the FIA of 'legitimizing dishonest behaviour' through a decision that was 'highly prejudicial to the credibility of the sport'. Ferrari centred their argument on the admission by the FIA that McLaren had been in breach of the motor sporting code thanks to having the Ferrari Documents in their possession.

Ron Dennis had been able to demonstrate that none of the information potentially available in the Ferrari dossier had either been used on their car or been absorbed into McLaren's method of racing. The council had to consider that any sanction would need to be significant, in which case it could seriously affect McLaren and, possibly, put the team out of business if they were excluded from the championship and sponsors withdrew.

After much deliberation, the council had decided that there was insufficient evidence to prove 'the unauthorized possession of documents and confidential information [that] could be used to design, engineer, build, check, test and develop their car'. The breach of the regulations alone (the act of possession caused by McLaren's collective responsibility over Coughlan) was not enough to warrant a draconian penalty. The council did add, however, that if it came to light that McLaren had been or were using information held illegally, then exclusion from both this and the 2008 championship would be inevitable. At the time, that seemed like a cover-all clause – mere legal jargon. In time, it would come to have a devastating effect on McLaren. But, for the moment, it did nothing to appease Ferrari.

Jean Todt claimed that McLaren had been told about certain aspects of the 2007 Ferrari as early as March and used that knowledge to draw the FIA's attention to the loophole which Ferrari were using to gain a performance advantage in Melbourne. Todt said: 'The McLaren bosses, with no exceptions, admitted [in court] that their chief designer had obtained in March documents from Nigel Stepney.' This contradicted Dennis's claim that he had no knowledge of this until 3 July. It was the first tiny chink in Dennis's highly polished armour.

The dispute appeared to have boiled down to the actions of two people: Coughlan and Stepney. Both men were under separate investigation and had been asked to explain themselves to the FIA. But the court case itself had brought to an end a most difficult twenty-four days in four decades of F1 involvement for Dennis. The Englishman claimed he had to rise above the innuendo and accusations as rivals attempted to use the occasion to destabilize his team. When he left the Paris courtroom, he said he was able to focus for the first time on the news that Hamilton had emerged as the fastest driver during a three-day test session at Jerez in Spain. Apart from preparing to continue his fight with Ferrari on the track in Hungary the following weekend, Dennis had the task of keeping everything civil within his own team after Alonso's victory in Germany had allowed the Spaniard to close to within 2 points of Hamilton.

Massa was back in third place but Räikkönen's retirement appeared to put the Ferrari driver out of the championship reckoning yet again as he trailed the leader by a massive 18 points. That was good news for Hamilton; despite not having scored points for the first time in 2007, he was still leading the championship. Twenty-one years before, and in the same country, Nigel Mansell had experienced similar feelings.

15
Mansell Miffed

Most motor sport fans in the 1960s had only a vague awareness of Hockenheim but that was to change on 7 April 1968. The German track became headline news in Britain as reports told the story of Jim Clark's death. The modest world champion from Scotland had been killed in a Formula Two race that most people knew even less about than the circuit located to the south of Mannheim. Clark's Lotus had been torn in two after it had left the track and crashed into trees that were completely unguarded. That summed up the primitive safety standards of the day and did nothing for Hockenheim's reputation as a flat and very fast track with little to say for itself.

The original track had run from the edge of the small town of Hockenheim, into a woodland and back again along very long straights. When a motorway cut its way across the bottom half of the track in 1966, the owners had used the compensation to build a massive concrete stadium and pit and paddock complex at the truncated end of the original track. This arena, particularly when packed with more than 100,000 spectators, added a much-needed sense of vitality. When concerns about safety on the original 14-mile Nürburgring forced the German Grand Prix to switch to Hockenheim in 1970, there was little enthusiasm for the move. In the event, the teams and fans were to be rewarded with a gripping contest between the Ferrari of Belgium's Jacky Ickx and the Lotus of the eventual winner and champion elect, Jochen

Chequered Conflict

Rindt. That eased the way for Hockenheim to become more or less the permanent home for the German Grand Prix in the 1980s.

Given that the neat market town was no more than a six-hour dash along autoroutes from the French coast, the circuit's stadium section had a reasonable sprinkling of British fans pledging support for Nigel Mansell in 1986. Having come off the back of two wins in France and Britain, Mansell continued to head the points table. But, when he reached the podium again in Germany, the Englishman knew he had been very fortunate to get that far.

With refuelling banned and the tank of each car limited to 195 litres, fuel efficiency was just as important as out-and-out speed. An economy run masquerading as a Grand Prix may not have been ideal but, just as the engine change restrictions caused frustration in 2007, these were the rules.

Prost had run out of fuel when lying third on the last lap. His team-mate, Keke Rosberg, suffered a similar problem and dropped from second to fifth, leaving Senna the grateful recipient as he moved into second place. Prost's indignation had been made public on the final corner when his McLaren stuttered to a halt in front of the huge grandstand. The Frenchman leaped out and, in a heroic gesture, tried to push his car the last few hundred metres to the line. But he gave up in disgust when he realized such a thing was not allowed and Mansell breezed by to move from fifth to third within sight of the flag. Both McLaren drivers were livid, Prost's comments summing up the mood as they came to terms with the effects of the fuel restrictions and inaccurate read-outs in the cockpit.

'Minimum [turbo] boost from the start,' said Prost. 'Sit there all afternoon, looking at the gauge. Then find the gauge is wrong, run out, push. You might as well have robots driving the cars in a race like this.'

Despite his windfall of 2 points, Mansell's set expression said everything about the identity of the driver on the top of the podium. After suffering at the hands of Mansell at the previous two races, Piquet had totally dominated this one. When Mansell had offered his hand in congratulations in parc fermé, Piquet had rudely ignored it. With ten rounds of the championship completed and another six to go, Mansell was 7 points ahead of Prost, with Senna a further 2 points behind and Piquet closing to within 4 of his fellow Brazilian. Mansell was more relieved than overjoyed. Two weeks later, he would be back on the podium – but deeply unhappy about having been denied, in his view, a fair chance to reach the top step.

F1 broke important new ground on 10 August 1986. Bernie Ecclestone, the driving force behind almost everything to do with F1, had been looking for some time to move the sport into communist countries. An attempt to raise interest in Moscow had got as far as serious talks but the project floundered on a technicality. Hungary, with its more liberal attitudes, then received Ecclestone's attention once he had visited the dignified city of Budapest.

Ecclestone found the necessary infrastructure in place: an international airport, good hotels, a reasonable communications system and, most important, an efficient television network. A proposed circuit through a park on the edge of the city – scene of the one previous Hungarian Grand Prix in 1936 – was rejected eventually on environmental grounds. But the Hungarians were aware of the importance of staging a televised major international event and raising the profile of a country saddled with a grey image and memories of the fearful uprising in 1956. A dusty and barren site twelve miles north-east of the capital was chosen and final approval granted in January 1985. Seventeen months later, the F1 teams rolled into Hungary and headed for the Hungaroring. The 2.5-mile track had been built at a cost of £5.3 million, a trifle by today's standards but a considerable investment by Forma-1, a new company consisting of several large businesses, each member having contributed 11 million florints (£170,000) to supplement an interest-free loan from the State Development Bank.

The track may have been tight and twisting but the organization was willing and enthusiastic. There had been doubts that the £13 admission charge would prove too steep for Hungarians earning on average £75 per month (a professional person's salary rising to £200 per month). An attendance in excess of 200,000 dispelled any fears of failure. The ranks of local people new to F1 were swollen by enthusiasts from Austria, East and West Germany and Czechoslovakia. The race, regardless of the circuit's limitations on overtaking, would provide the necessary entertainment.

Senna, with a typically daring lap, had claimed pole, ahead of Piquet and Mansell, with Prost sixth fastest after struggling to make the McLaren work. Frank Williams, who had managed to make the trip to Hungary, was probably relieved to see Piquet the quicker of his two drivers. Following defeat at Brands Hatch, where he thought Mansell had been heavy-handed in his driving tactics, Piquet had complained to Williams. A story leaked out that the Brazilian had been tearful while telling the boss his woes. If that was true, then Piquet was to employ a more devious tactic on the track in Hungary.

Piquet, while experimenting with the differential on his car, discovered that the revised transmission produced a considerable performance advantage by making the car more manageable through the many tight corners of the Hungaroring. Unfortunately, he somehow forgot to share this knowledge with the rest of the team, keeping the information a secret between him and his engineer. Such a thing would never occur today. Every moving aspect of a racing car is monitored electronically in great detail and any changes would be obvious to all concerned within the team. At the likes of McLaren, even the smallest change to a car would be on the table during engineering debriefs between Alonso, Hamilton and their respective engineers.

In 1986, neither driver was required to share their findings. Mansell became aware that something was different about Piquet's car when the Brazilian lapped him during the race – while leading comfortably. This was humiliation of the worst kind, particularly for a driver with a persecution complex that would surface at the merest bidding. When a beaming Piquet climbed on to the top of the podium, with Senna having finished second, a grim-faced Mansell could barely speak with rage as he stood alongside. He had been stitched up. Nigel knew it and, of course, so did Nelson. Prost, who had been eliminated in a collision, had dropped to fourth behind Piquet on the points table. Mansell still led. But you would never have known it.

The Hungarian Grand Prix had arrived in style as an international race but it had driven a wedge between the Williams drivers. Twenty-one years later, exactly the same thing would happen, this time within McLaren. In a season of many incidents and memories, the 2007 Hungarian Grand Prix would stand out as a catalyst for distrust and bitterness the like of which had rarely been witnessed before. It would make Piquet's dabbling with the differential a mere bagatelle.

16

Credibility Crash

McLaren's world fell apart completely in Hungary and Lewis Hamilton, the team's blue-eyed boy, helped trigger some of the internal bitterness. In a business devoted to moving quickly, it seemed fitting that the McLaren team should suddenly self-destruct because their cars were standing still. In the 10 seconds it would take Fernando Alonso to hold up Hamilton in the pit lane during qualifying at the Hungaroring, McLaren's carefully managed image and modus operandi would collapse in an undignified heap thanks to the actions of two of the team's highest-paid employees. The fact that other team members on a modest wage looked like suffering a loss of income as a result was one of the many ironies surrounding this latest unexpected development in a season that was already being noted for its exceptional occurrences.

Ron Dennis will remember the Hungarian Grand Prix for reasons other than his team's 153rd victory as Hamilton held off Räikkönen's Ferrari for 70 laps. In fact, the events in Budapest were so catastrophic for McLaren that they achieved the seemingly impossible by pushing – temporarily, at least – the Ferrari spy scandal into the margins.

Trouble began during qualifying at the beginning of the third and final phase, Q3. A recap of the rules is appropriate at this point. For Q3, each car had to start with the same amount of fuel intended for the beginning of the race. (The original idea was to introduce a tactical element as well as variety to qualifying by allowing a driver who wished to run with a light load of fuel to qualify on pole in the knowledge that there would be a price to pay as he would have to make his first refuelling stop early in the race. In the end, of course, the teams quickly discovered that there was only one optimum choice and each driver ended up running more or less the same amount of fuel.) Once qualifying had finished, each car would be replenished. But the fuel added would be calculated by a predetermined amount for each of the laps completed during Q3.

The natural inclination for a driver, let us call him Driver A, would be to burn off as much fuel as possible in order to have the car at its minimum weight when fresh tyres were fitted for the final lap of qualifying. Driver B might prefer to be economical during the opening laps of the 15-minute Q3 session. That way, Driver B, who would have done the same number of laps as Driver A, would actually use less fuel than he was about to be credited for at the end, thus putting more fuel in the tank and allowing a longer and tactically more beneficial first phase of the race.

Having each driver run a different strategy also helped the team operationally – and this was significant in a qualifying session timed and planned to the last second. If both drivers went flat out during Q3 then the cars would arrive at the pits together for their final sets of tyres. By having one car run slightly more slowly then, with a couple of minutes to go before the end of the 15-minute session, there would be a gap of at least 10 seconds between the cars, thus allowing the crew to fit new tyres without the unnecessary rush caused by having one car queuing behind the other. Also, by putting less fuel in Driver B's car at the start (because he would be more economical) then, in theory, both drivers would have the same amount on board when it came to the final lap of qualifying, thus ensuring equality.

McLaren had always been scrupulous when alternating the

tactics between drivers in order to be fair to both during the course of the season. For Hungary, it was agreed that Alonso would go first and drive flat out from the start of Q3 while Hamilton would save fuel by running a couple of seconds a lap slower for the first 6 laps.

It all began to go wrong when Hamilton was the first to arrive at the end of the pit lane a few minutes before the start of Q3. On the green light, Hamilton shot on to the track. Despite being reminded by the team to allow Alonso to overtake, Hamilton appeared not to heed the instruction. Hamilton would later claim that Alonso was not following closely enough and he did not want to slow unnecessarily in case Räikkönen, in close attendance in his Ferrari, slipped past as well.

It soon became apparent to Alonso that he was not going to be in a position to go flat out. Instead, he went into fuel-save mode. Hamilton, having less fuel on board (because he was due to be economical during the first 6 laps), put the hammer down. Now he had the best of both worlds: a light car and burning off the maximum amount of fuel. The penalty would be stopping early in the race but, because of overtaking difficulties at the Hungaroring, pole position would be paramount: Hamilton would sort everything else out later. But that was before Alonso had the last word.

Alonso made his final stop first. Tyres were fitted and he was held by the mechanic with the 'lollipop' positioned in front of the cockpit and controlling the driver's exit from the McLaren pit box. When the lollipop was lifted, Alonso remained stationary. Then Hamilton arrived for his last-minute change of tyres.

'When I was coming into the pits, I was told Fernando was making his stop and I was told to back off,' said Hamilton. 'So, I saved a bit of time but then I saw that Fernando was still there, the tyres were on and he was ready to go. I didn't know why he was being held there.'

Hamilton was not alone. The watching television audience

was baffled, particularly when Alonso eventually set off and managed to cross the line in time to start his final lap. Meanwhile, Hamilton had been delayed just enough to prevent him from crossing the start/finish line before the chequered flag appeared. Alonso was on pole with Hamilton alongside. Now the recriminations began.

Dennis could be seen ripping off his headset and marching towards the end of the pit lane, where the cars would come to a halt. His mind was in a whirl. He had experienced his young protégé kicking the traces when Hamilton failed to follow the agreed strategy at the start of qualifying. Then Alonso, as a reprisal, appeared to have taken the law into his hands by waiting for 10 seconds after his stop had ostensibly been completed. On his slowing down lap, Hamilton was reported to have used strong language – a fact later denied by both the driver and the team – when telling Dennis what he thought of the delay in the pits. No one outside McLaren knew any of this. All that could be seen was Hamilton having a terse conversation with Dennis while Alonso completely ignored them both. Something was clearly amiss but, at this stage, observers could only speculate on the cause of the problem.

Both McLarens may have been on the front row but Hamilton's displeasure was generated by the thought that he would be starting the eleventh round of the championship from a position that was off the racing line and on the dirtier side of the track. This was a crucial development for Hamilton since overtaking on this track would be even more difficult than usual.

It also came at a critical point in the championship. Hamilton had seen his lead slashed from 12 points to 2 when he failed to score for the first time at the Nürburgring two weeks before and Alonso won the race. There were six rounds remaining after the Hungarian race and another win for Alonso would give the reigning world champion a psychological advantage.

McLaren had scheduled their usual 'Meet the Team' media

debriefing after qualifying and, in the light of the bewildering events during qualifying, a full attendance in the Brand Centre was guaranteed. In a desperate bid to maintain calm and an impression of even-handedness, Dennis would actually make things worse.

He began by apologizing for the absence of Hamilton, saying he was 'too hot' to take part; a reference, it was assumed, to his driver still being angry over the delay in the pit lane. Alonso, nonchalantly chewing a pear and sitting to the right of Dennis, looked straight ahead while Dennis attempted to explain what had happened. He revealed that Hamilton had failed to let Alonso through at the start of Q3, an action that immediately upset the planned pit-stop sequence during the final phase of qualifying. This was the first anyone outside the team knew of Hamilton's uncharitable behaviour.

Dennis then explained that a driver is held in the pit box until his engineer figures the time is right to release the car on to a clear piece of track. This, according to Dennis, was why Alonso had been stationary for 20 seconds. When asked if this was correct, Alonso nodded, gave a thumbs up but continued to chew his pear and stare straight ahead rather than look Dennis in the eye. It was difficult to say whether Alonso's behaviour was the work of an over-active guilt complex or the fact that what he was hearing did not tally exactly with the facts.

Dennis then received a call to go before the stewards, leaving Alonso on his own to fend off questions from the media. No sooner had he started than Alonso was joined by Hamilton, who apologized and explained his lateness by saying he had lost track of time while watching the GP2 support race. The intensity of the questions grew in direct proportion to the variation in answers from the drivers. Hamilton said he regretted going against team orders at the start of Q3 but he then contradicted Alonso by claiming that he always took the raising of the lollipop as the signal to leave the pits rather than through a countdown from his engineer. Without the presence of Dennis as referee, the press conference became more chaotic and heated by the moment. Watching proceedings with growing alarm from an upper gallery, Martin Whitmarsh dashed downstairs and called an immediate halt to the conference, much to the relief of Alonso who had become visibly annoyed. The press conference had descended into chaos, not helped by McLaren and Mercedes-Benz having their respective press officers take holiday leave at the same race. But at least the media had some answers. Or so it seemed.

Many of the journalists had previously felt that Alonso had acted on his own initiative by deliberately delaying Hamilton as a reprisal. Dennis had clarified this by saying the team had kept Alonso in the pits. That was how Hamilton had been prevented from rejoining the track in time to do one more lap and be the fastest driver, just as he had been quickest more or less since the start of practice the previous day. I was not alone in accepting these facts at face value and passing them on to the outside world.

Early that evening, BBC Radio 5 Live held a sixty-minute discussion programme to which listeners were invited to send emails and texts. The majority of correspondents were of the opinion that Alonso was, at best, a naughty boy and, at worst, an irresponsible deviant not worthy of office as world champion. From a position of so-called authority, I was able to put them right, explaining Hamilton's part in the proceedings and the influence of the team over Alonso's apparent dilatory behaviour in the pit lane. By the following morning, the true story had begun to emerge.

Yes, Hamilton had disregarded the agreed plan at the start of Q3. But Dennis's explanation about Alonso's behaviour, while not being a lie, had been short of the truth. Closer examination of the statistics showed that there was only a handful of cars on the track, thus placing doubt on the team's need to hold their driver for so long. But, significantly, Dennis had omitted to say that Alonso had actually been at a standstill for half a minute, the final 10 seconds having been Alonso's doing and not the team's. Now it was clear that Dennis had been economical with the facts in a desperate bid to be seen to be fair and not criticize Alonso after he had been upset by Hamilton's actions.

In the space of two hours on the Saturday afternoon, Dennis had learned a shocking amount about the steely character of Hamilton and how this golden boy had suddenly come of age. The media were to be equally surprised and disappointed by the appearance of cracks in Dennis's integrity as he declined to admit that Alonso had taken the law into his own hands. Knowing the values placed by Dennis on honourable behaviour, it was difficult to know which development had upset him most.

Meanwhile, it took the race stewards five hours to study videos, listen to some, but not all, of McLaren's radio transmissions and hear statements. Quite why the officials had to become involved in what amounted to a domestic dispute was a mystery. It was suggested that either Hamilton or his father, Anthony, had asked the stewards for clarification over whether something could be done about a driver deliberately delaying his teammate in the pit lane.

The stewards decided to penalize Alonso five places on the grid as well as preventing both drivers from scoring team points on Sunday. For Hamilton, the first was good news since it moved him on to the pole position he felt would have been rightfully his. But the latter declaration was a shock since, strictly speaking, Hamilton had triggered the entire affair and now the McLaren mechanics would miss out on bonus money that should have accompanied any points earned in the race. By all accounts, some mechanics were not slow in making their feelings known on the subject.

On race morning, Hamilton began to rebuild broken bridges by speaking to each team member in turn. According to

Hamilton, only two people (one of whom could have been Alonso) refused to shake his hand. However, if Hamilton thought he had his troubles as he toured the garage, Dennis was about to experience an unprecedented and unbelievable reaction as he and Alonso met in the Brand Centre.

Alonso had been deeply upset by a grid penalty that had been aggravated by Hamilton escaping without punishment. In Alonso's mind, this was yet another demonstration of how the McLaren team was favouring the wrong driver. In his view, this had gone far enough. Alonso threatened to reveal the content of emails on his laptop showing Ferrari information if Dennis did not provide the preferential treatment that Alonso continued to believe was his due. Alonso said he would act if Dennis refused to either keep Hamilton in check or go as far as engineering a problem with his team-mate's car.

Dennis was stunned. Never, in more than forty years in motor sport, had a driver threatened to blackmail, not only the boss, but also the entire team. And, in any case, Dennis knew nothing about the emails which, it would turn out, had been sent earlier in the year between Pedro de la Rosa and Alonso as they discussed information which, according to the Spanish drivers, had come from Nigel Stepney, via Mike Coughlan. If this were true, then it would blow wide open Dennis's heavily recited defence that only Coughlan had used the Ferrari information and none of it had fallen into the hands of other team members.

Alonso later retracted his angry words but not before Dennis had informed the FIA of this development in his spirit of openness and honesty. Sensing McLaren were more deeply involved in the Ferrari scandal than Dennis had earlier claimed, the FIA reconvened the World Motor Sport Council for 13 September. The can of worms, bigger and more active this time, had just been reopened. Meanwhile, there was a race to be won.

Ferrari's chances in Hungary had been badly damaged when the team, in a rare error of judgement, had sent Massa away from the pits without adding fuel during qualifying. By the time the car had been pushed back to the pits, the tyre temperatures had dropped and the Brazilian was unable to improve on fourteenth place. This was the worst possible circuit for such a delay. At the start, Massa did his cause no good by letting the Super Aguri of Takuma Sato get the jump on him, Massa remaining stuck behind the Japanese car for the first phase of the race. The Brazilian eventually finished out of the points in ninth place at the end of a desperately disappointing afternoon.

Räikkönen, meanwhile, gave Ferrari some consolation as he moved from third on the grid and took second from Heidfeld's BMW, Räikkönen then chasing Hamilton for 1 hour and 35 minutes. Hamilton did not put a foot wrong despite such pressure, Räikkönen admitting there was little he could do if Hamilton failed to make a mistake. Alonso, meanwhile, had been trapped behind Ralf Schumacher for the first 50 laps, the very unhappy Spaniard eventually moving ahead of the Toyota to finish fourth.

It was clear from Hamilton's uncharacteristic discomfort at the post-race press conference that events of the previous twenty-four hours were continuing to weigh heavily. The difficulties with Alonso aside, the financial penalty affecting the mechanics was adding to discord within a team that Dennis liked to depict as being united by strong core values. Looking emotionally drained after the race, Dennis insisted McLaren would carry on as before. 'We will continue to function as a Grand Prix team with specific values,' said Dennis. 'If anybody does not want to be part of those values – irrespective of where they sit in the organization – ultimately they all have a choice.'

Alonso, despite having a further two years to run on his contract, now seemed certain to exercise that choice sooner rather than later. Alonso's perceived lack of respect for his status had not been helped by Hamilton occasionally making the double world champion look average. Dennis had gone out of his way to avoid inaccurate accusations of favouritism towards Hamilton – the vigorous and marginally disingenuous defence of Alonso's pit lane behaviour being a case in point – but that did not look like being enough to persuade Alonso to stay.

In the meantime, Hamilton and Alonso needed to learn to coexist. Despite Hamilton's assurance that stories of open hostility were as inaccurate as reports that he swore at Dennis over the radio, the Englishman now knew that Alonso would stop at nothing to win a third successive title, particularly if he planned to make a premature departure from the team. Equally, Alonso had become dramatically aware that Hamilton was now ploughing his own furrow, preferably across the Spaniard's path.

st appearance. Elio de Angelis hustles the low-line Brabham-BMW through a chicane at ˙naco. The Italian was killed a few days later during a test session in France, the last ˙ality in F1 until 1994.

plays Motown. Ayrton Senna talks to his engineer, Steve Hallam (yellow cap), during ˙actice in Detroit. The glass towers of the Renaissance Centre overlook the open pits on the ˙mporary circuit. Hallam would be a key member of the McLaren technical team overseeing ˙rnando Alonso and Lewis Hamilton in 2007.

Let's party. The Detroit Grand Prix was always popular with race fans, many of whom seemed to be in the pit lane. Ayrton Senna leads from pole on his way to a second win in 1986 and a temporary place at the top of the championship. Nigel Mansell, starting from the front row, is destined to finish fifth. Alain Prost would eventually come through from seventh on the grid to take third.

Back where he belongs. Nigel Mansell and Nelson Piquet pose with Frank Williams on the return of their boss to F1 following his debilitating accident.

Tall car, low fuel. The McLaren-TAG seems huge by today's standards. Alain Prost did a typically clever job by eking out the maximum of 195 litres of fuel to finish second in Portugal and keep his championship hopes alive.

hoto missed opportunity. The four contenders of 1986 – (l to r) Ayrton Senna, Alain Prost, gel Mansell and Nelson Piquet – pose for a group photograph on the pit wall at Estoril. An tempt to stage a repeat photo call with the leaders in 2007 was blocked by one of the ams.

role model. James Hunt (left) caused a stir when the 1976 world champion suggested it ould not be popular within F1 if Nigel Mansell became the next Englishman to win the title.

Don't leave me this way. Nigel Mansell (5) looks on helplessly as the Mexican Grand Prix starts without him after the Williams driver failed to find first gear. Mansell was poised to win the title at this penultimate round. Lewis Hamilton would be in the same position 21 years later.

That's blown it! Nigel Mansell brings his Williams-Honda to a halt in Adelaide.

pintless exercise. To sympathetic applause, a stunned Nigel Mansell ends his season with a nely walk back to the pits in Adelaide.

ever give up. Alain Prost's championship seemed to have gone the way of the air from his unctured front tyre. The McLaren mechanics are dressed in waterproof capes even though did not rain. In 1986, there was no refuelling (hence the absence of helmets and flame-oof gear) and only two mechanics instead of the three per wheel that make up a team of 3 people tending to the McLaren-Mercedes each time it stops. This stop to change the ght-front wheel took 17 seconds. In 2007, the car with a similar problem would have been spatched in less than six seconds.

Making a connection. Happy days as Fernando Alonso and Lewis Hamilton take part in a pre-season press call on Melbourne's St Kilda Beach.

Flattering to deceive. Kimi Raikkonen's dominant win at the first race in Melbourne gave the impression that 2007 would be a Ferrari walk-over. Raikkonen would not win again until the French Grand Prix in July.

ollow my leader. Lewis Hamilton slots in behind Fernando Alonso as the leaders squeeze
rough the first corner at Monaco. Felipe Massa follows closely while the second Ferrari of
1ampion-elect Kimi Raikkonen can be seen top right, near the back of the field, following
s indiscretion during qualifying.

MW in waiting. If McLaren and Ferrari slipped up, BMW were ready and willing to
apitalise. Nick Heidfeld follows Lewis Hamilton at Monaco, the white stripes in the grooved
ridgestone tyres showing both drivers to be running the softer of the two options available.

Watch out behind you! Fernando Alonso may have lifted the winner's cup at Monaco but the reigning world champion felt his flawless weekend had been tainted by Lewis Hamilton's complaints about team tactics.

Who, me? Ferrari's Nigel Stepney kicked off a season of unprecedented controversy in 2007.

Numero Uno. Lewis Hamilton, on top of the world in Canada.

Unbelievable! The 1986 World Champion celebrates his second consecutive title. Nelson Piquet, who would have won but for a tyre change, is on Alain Prost's right. Stefan Johansson finished third for Ferrari. Note Prost's relatively sponsor-free overalls compared to those of Lewis Hamilton 21 years later.

What a feeling. Lewis Hamilton clutches his trophy (made in Northern Ireland from Tyrone Crystal) after his first grand prix win in Montreal.

Ridiculously safe. Robert Kubica's BMW clatters to a halt after multiple-impacts so severe that the Polish driver's feet were exposed after the front of the car had been torn off. Kubica was unhurt.

No way through. Fernando Alonso (left) was unable to overtake Lewis Hamilton for the lead at Indianapolis, not even after asking for the team's assistance.

Wielding the wheel. Kimi Raikkonen finds another task for his Ferrari's multipurpose steering wheel at Silverstone as he acknowledges the plaudits for his second win in succession.

Doubling up. Felipe Massa's image on both cups reflects his second dominant win in succession in Turkey as the Brazilian keeps his championship hopes alive.

Getting to grips. Once he had settled in at Ferrari and become accustomed to the characteristics of the Bridgestone tyres, Kimi Raikkonen recovered from a poor opening third of the season with consistently fast and strong drives.

Eye of the storm. Max Mosley, in his role as president of the FIA, is pressed for answers during a season in which politics dominated from the first race of 2007 until the last – and beyond.

Trust me; you have my word. Ron Dennis addresses reporters outside an FIA court in Paris The credibility of the McLaren boss was badly dented during the extraordinary events of 2007.

hrashed. Fernando Alonso abandons his McLaren during the Japanese Grand Prix after a istake that damaged both his car and his championship chances.

ublime skill. Lewis Hamilton scored a significant and arguably his best victory with a superb ive in atrocious conditions in Japan.

Treadbare. A disbelieving Hamilton walks away from his McLaren after sliding into the gravel trap at the entrance to the pit lane in Shanghai. Exposed canvas on the McLaren's right-rear tyre tells the story.

Stitched up. Lewis Hamilton is boxed in by the Ferraris as the field streams into the first corner at Interlagos. Fernando Alonso is ready to pounce on his McLaren team-mate a few seconds later when Hamilton is further delayed on the downhill run to the second corner.

hat's m'boy!' Jean Todt congratulates Kimi Raikkonen on his 11th-hour victory and the
hampionship. Fernando Alonso enjoyed second place and, probably, the thought that
ewis Hamilton's title hopes ended in failure.

Iceman. Kimi Raikkonen steered
clear of the politics, maintained his
self-confidence, won more races
than anyone else and thoroughly
deserved his first world title.

Lord of all he surveys? Max Mosley frequently caused as much controversy during 2007 as the teams he was attempting to control.

The fat lady finally sings. After the legal arguments had been settled, Kimi Raikkonen and Jean Todt picked up the winning driver's and constructor's trophies at the FIA prize giving in Monte Carlo.

17
Everyone's a Winner

The Austrian Grand Prix was struck from the calendar in 2004. Its removal was met with mixed feelings. The majestic natural beauty of the surroundings did not make up for the circuit's remote location or a layout that was a butchered version of the original. The first Österreichring had been carved out of the foothills of a mountain range overlooking the provincial town of Zeltweg. Introduced as a round of the world championship in 1970, the 3.7-mile track impressed everyone, not least the drivers when they realized what was required to reach an average lap speed of 131 m.p.h. From the outset, the Österreichring had a sense of presence and maturity, the owners having used the rolling terrain to full advantage. The corners were fast and many of them were blind. In this day and age, Lewis Hamilton would not be allowed to race a kart, never mind a F1 car, on something similar.

The Bosch Kurve, a perfectly cambered downhill right-hander, was an awesome example of the challenge. Approaching at close to 200 m.p.h., drivers would dab the brakes, shift down a gear and then apply the power as soon as they dared while barrelling into the swooping curve. This corner, and others like it, required a combination of bravery and skill. With a barrier waiting right on the edge at the exit, nothing could be left to chance.

A reminder of the ever-present danger had come during the morning warm-up for the 1975 Grand Prix. The Hella-Licht

157

Chequered Conflict

Kurve was a very fast right-hander at the top of the hill above the pits. A tyre problem on Mark Donohue's March meant the American failed to take the corner. Catch-fencing (wire mesh supported by small poles designed to give way on impact) was supposed to arrest the progress of a wayward car. In this instance, Donohue mowed down several layers of mesh but the speed was such that the fencing gathered beneath the car and raised it high enough to clear the crash barrier. The March severely injured two marshals and then slammed into steel poles supporting an advertising hoarding. Donohue caught a sharp blow to the head. Although conscious before being helicoptered to hospital, he died a few days later.

A chicane was inserted at the Hella-Licht but the challenge and splendour of the place remained when the F1 teams crossed the border from Hungary for the Austrian Grand Prix in 1986. With only a week having passed since the previous race, Mansell remained miffed about the behaviour of his team-mate.

Piquet had arrived at Williams expecting to be the dominant driver, much as Alonso would do at McLaren in 2007. Piquet's fee of $3.3 million reflected his two world championships and thirteen wins. Mansell, earning considerably less, had just two victories to his name at the beginning of the season. Piquet had no reason to doubt that this would be 'his' team when he won the first race in Brazil after Mansell had crashed on the first lap. When Mansell almost won in Spain, however, Piquet laid down the law. Williams, in common with other leading teams of the day, brought just one spare car to each race. This was to be alternated between the drivers and it had been Mansell's turn to have the use of two cars in Spain. Piquet had immediately stamped on that arrangement, demanding the spare car for himself on an ongoing basis, an asset he had used to the full when experimenting with the differential settings in Hungary. The point had not been lost on Mansell, who was quick to point out that he, and not Piquet, was leading the championship:

It's a bit restricting having just the one car. You can make a lot more progress if you've two cars to work with. I've noticed that when Nelson's been in trouble getting the set-up right in practice, he and his engineer have sometimes looked at my car and transferred the settings to his. That doesn't bother me – after all, it means that Piquet ends up with a car set up for me. I've also noticed that he only seems to talk about the cars when he wants to.

The precise ownership of the spare car would not help either Williams driver as they struggled for straight-line speed in Austria, Mansell qualifying sixth, one place ahead of Piquet. For the one and only time in 1986, the front row was occupied by a pair of Benettons, the fast sections of the track allowing the very powerful BMW turbo engine to make up for deficiencies within the rest of the car. Under the rules of the day, the F1 cars were missiles on this sort of track. With 1-lap qualifying tyres allowed, the sticky rubber, dealing with as much as 1400 b.h.p. thanks to maximum turbo boost, would give the drivers a feeling of limitless power and performance. The fact that one of the colourful Benettons was driven by an Austrian, Gerhard Berger, seemed to catch the locals by surprise, the attendance being poor by recent standards.

Berger would have his moment in the sun as he led a Grand Prix for the first time and held that position for 25 laps. Then the battery went flat; one of the silly things that happened before the rigorous quality control and electronic monitoring evident today. The 1986 Austrian Grand Prix was a case in point. After just 15 of the 52 laps, eleven of the twenty-six starters had been eliminated. It was true that the flat-out nature of the track was stretching machinery to the limit and would eventually cause ten engine and turbo-related failures. But, from a championship point of view, more significant was the inclusion on the retirement list of Senna and Piquet – soon to be joined by Mansell. Berger's retirement had let Mansell into the lead after the Williams driver had made a good start and gradually moved up the order. A pit stop dropped Mansell behind Prost but the Englishman would disappear completely when a driveshaft broke.

Prost, his fuel consumption presenting no problems on this occasion, was looking good. Or so he thought. With 4 laps to go, the TAG-Porsche V6 cut out at the Hella-Licht chicane. Prost bump-started the engine and continued. Two laps later, it happened again at the very same place, the engine dying as Prost came off the throttle for the slowest corner on the track. This had caught the attention of the sizeable Italian contingent in the crowd. Catching Prost hand over fist were the Ferraris of Michele Alboreto and Stefan Johansson. A double podium finish would be more than welcome during a miserable season for the uncompetitive Italian team; a one–two would be almost unbelievable.

'Eventually,' said Prost, 'I thought it was going to die for good. I knew that. It was happening every time I braked. I had to use the gearbox much more for slowing. Then the engine started to misfire – sometimes it even cut out in the middle of the straight, just like it had done in Hungary. I really thought I would not get to the finish.'

In fact, he would stutter across the line, saved by the fact that the Ferraris were a lap behind. Prost's change in fortune after two retirements moved him into second place in the championship, 2 points behind Mansell and 5 ahead of Senna and Piquet.

Average speeds had risen to 150 m.p.h. despite the inclusion of the Hella-Licht chicane. Events during the 1987 race would sum up mounting problems for the Österreichring as a series of collisions on the narrow pit straight would mean two aborted starts before the Grand Prix got under way. Mansell won it that year but, even then, the Englishman somehow added to the increasingly unusual aspect of the place.

On the first day of practice, Mansell had insisted on clutching a bag of ice to his jaw and showing an extracted tooth to anyone foolish enough to ask about his problem. Then, having overcome this fearsome physical handicap on race day, Mansell almost knocked himself out when he stood up at the wrong moment and struck his head on an iron girder as the jeep bringing the winner from parc fermé drove through an entry in the pit buildings. When Murray Walker carelessly poked the injured famous forehead while interviewing Mansell on BBC TV, the comedy was complete. So was the future of the Österreichring in that form. A truncated and sanitized version was introduced in 1997 and lasted for seven years. The absence of the Österreichring left a hole in the calendar that was neatly filled by a new venue in Turkey in 2005 even though the two locations could not have been more extreme.

18
Stirring the Turkish Pot

Designed by Hermann Tilke, Istanbul Park broke away from some of the German architect's more tedious designs by introducing elevation change to help produce blind, challenging corners. Tilke then accidentally hit on a novel method of making future circuits as tricky as this one. Having followed the usual pattern of penning the layout to run in a clockwise direction, Tilke realized that Istanbul Park might actually be more interesting if used in the reverse direction to the one originally intended. At the time, that meant Istanbul would join Imola and Interlagos as the only anti-clockwise tracks in the series, a novelty that brings problems for neck muscles accustomed to circuits with a predominant number of right-hand corners. Significantly, the most difficult corner of the lot, turn 8, went left in a long and bumpy arc that would seek out muscular weakness. Istanbul Park was considered to be worthy of its place on the calendar as the 2007 contenders travelled to Turkey for the eleventh round of an increasingly bitter contest.

There had been a break of two free weekends. Both McLaren drivers had been invited to spend time on a boat belonging to Mansour Ojjeh, a long-time partner in McLaren and good friend of Ron Dennis. Hamilton accepted the offer but Alonso declined. Hamilton spent the week in the Mediterranean relaxing with Ojjeh's family and friends. Having thought he had got away from it all, Hamilton returned ashore to find that the long lenses of the paparazzi had never been far away. Worse still, photographs of Hamilton and Ojjeh's 18-year-old daughter, Sara, were splashed across the tabloids, accompanied by stories probing his love life. As soon as he reached the paddock in Istanbul, Hamilton was keen to set the record straight:

> I'm not a playboy. I haven't gone out and bought lots of expensive cars, I'm not dating all these women. If I was, then fair play and write stuff about me. But I'm just trying to lead a normal life. All those stories are completely wrong.
>
> I was supposed to go away with my friends, with the lads and have a lads' holiday, but I thought it was a bad idea at the mid part of the season where I'm leading the championship. I thought it was better just to relax, do some training and I was invited on to the boat and they took care of me – there were thirteen of us on the boat and there were three of the Ojjeh daughters and they all had their boyfriends there.
>
> When I first got there, I wasn't expecting to have pictures taken of us and what you don't see in that picture is that there were twelve of us in the back of the boat throwing each other in. At the end of the day, it probably wouldn't be so bad if I was getting together with all these women, but I'm not. I just found out the other day that I've slept with [pop singer] Dido. I don't remember it.

Hamilton said the media intrusion into his private life had affected others close to him, particularly the implication that he was cheating on his former girlfriend.

> My ex-girlfriend and I are still great friends and we talk all the time but the papers just keep on bringing that up. It's devastating for both of us. Now I am supposedly dating one of the Ojjehs, which is completely untrue. She has a boyfriend. We are just great friends.

Then I went to the cinema the other day with my best friend and his fiancée and my friend Mohammed. The papers said one of them was my bodyguard and I'm seeing this girl. So now I'm cheating on someone else.

Having established the truth about his private life, Hamilton then turned to the more pressing business of F1 and his relationship with the team. Rather than get together under the glare of publicity at the racetrack, Ron Dennis decided to avoid the twenty-five-mile journey from the centre of Istanbul and have the drivers meet in private at their hotel in an attempt to clear the air. They had not spoken since the shambles in Hungary. Hamilton described their meeting as 'really relaxed and chilled'. Hamilton explained:

I put my hands up and apologized for everything that went on at the last race, and Fernando said, 'Yeah, me too.' It was a discussion recognizing that we do have respect for each other. The respect is there no doubt. He said, 'I have no problems with you', and it is the same for me. I'm not saying that all of a sudden everything is bright, but we've come back and all settled our differences and where we want to go.

The team and myself want to move forward, so we've put it all in the past. I feel very comfortable and confident that we both have the opportunity to go out and battle each other. That's what racing is all about. Things are looking better, a lot better than you would imagine after the last race when everything went as bad as it could ever be.

A lot of that is from the press who are always writing stories about me and Fernando being at war. It obviously sells a lot more papers, but we are not at war. We are both extremely competitive drivers wanting to win the world championship, but that doesn't deter us from the fact that we respect each other and want to get on.

Ron has had a good holiday as well and has had time to reflect on his actions and it is the same for me and Fernando. We have learned from our lessons and I really feel so fresh coming into this race. I spoke to a lot of people at the team and they feel we have turned over a new leaf. We have put it behind us and moved forwards and that is the most important thing.

Fernando and I addressed our issues that we have with the team and we have been assured that it is equal and we are having equal equipment and equal opportunities. We have to keep on pushing but the war is not between him and me. We have to work together as a team to get the constructors' and drivers' championship.

The fact is that we get on well. We don't have issues; we are not fighting, or wrestling each other. We are just two extremely competitive drivers. You cannot be best friends. It is always hard when you are competing against someone in your own team, but the fact is that we get on really well. After having all these discussions I just feel relaxed and that the team are moving forward.

That may have been the way Hamilton wanted to portray it, but Alonso continued to gently stir the pot during an interview with BBC Radio 5 Live:

That is always very clear in any team, you know, to have equal opportunities to everybody and to have an equal car to your team-mate. What I think sometimes, and what I asked the team, is that I gave the team a lot. When I arrived in December, I remember the car I drove; I remember the results they had in 2006. And now, you know, I brought to the team half a second, six tenths, whatever, and I don't see anything given me back.

That may have been a step backwards for relationships within McLaren but the British team needed to focus on the fact that Ferrari had taken a necessary step forward. After McLaren's recent success on track, it was essential for Ferrari, and Massa in particular, to set the record straight as the season moved into its final third.

For most of practice in Istanbul, Massa never really figured but, when it mattered most, the Brazilian suddenly produced a superb lap to take pole position. When Hamilton declared himself happy with second on the grid, it was difficult to tell whether his pleasure had been generated by suddenly finding a competitive lap time or the fact that he had qualified two places ahead of Alonso, Räikkönen's Ferrari splitting the two McLarens.

In the light of events during qualifying three weeks before in Hungary, Hamilton knew that Alonso was a potentially greater menace than the combined force of Ferrari. With the previous destructive gamesmanship during qualifying in mind, McLaren took the decision to provide each driver with a separate pit crew, Alonso further lessening the threat of a blockage in the pit lane by running a completely different strategy during qualifying and changing to fresh tyres long after Hamilton had made his stop.

If Hamilton had been the happy McLaren driver post-qualifying, then it was Alonso who wore the smile after the race when he finished third and knew he was fortunate to be there. A poor getaway had meant Alonso had been swamped by the pair of BMWs starting directly behind the McLaren. Down in sixth place, it was little consolation for Alonso to note that Hamilton had also made a comparatively slow start from the dirty side of the track, the Englishman being overhauled by Räikkönen to give Ferrari a one–two going into the first corner. As Alonso studied the back of Heidfeld's gearbox, the leading trio made their escape, Hamilton hanging on to the Ferraris.

Chequered Conflict

There was no doubt that the red cars had marginally better pace thanks, in part, to being able to make the softer tyres work during the opening stints while Hamilton had to make do with the harder version. (Bridgestone had, as usual, brought two different types of tyre – a hard and a soft – and the rules demanded that the drivers use each type at some stage during the race.) The only hope was that Hamilton could take advantage of having the soft tyre during his final of three stints while the Ferraris, as the rules required, would have to run the hard tyre. Hamilton never got the chance to try. Istanbul's turn 8 would have its say.

The long left-hander had, in a short space of time, already earned its place among the great names such as Eau Rouge at Spa, Becketts at Silverstone and Suzuka's 130R. Turn 8 has four apexes and a smattering of bumps to further unsettle a car as it sweeps through at 135 m.p.h. With the track temperature in excess of 50 degrees C, the right-front tyre was severely punished. As he came through turn 8 on lap 43, Hamilton noticed bits of rubber flying off the right-front. When he reached the braking area for turn 9, the Bridgestone delaminated suddenly and Hamilton was lucky not to hit the barrier as he shot into the run-off area. He was even more fortunate to limp back to the pits and recover to finish fifth behind Heidfeld.

Meanwhile, at the front, Räikkönen had been powerless to dislodge his team-mate from the lead. The Finn admitted that the race had more or less been settled when he got out of shape briefly during his qualifying lap, a mistake that ensured he would have the less favourable pit-stop sequence within Ferrari. 'There's nothing you can do after that,' said Räikkönen. 'Felipe didn't make any mistakes. I got a bit bored towards the end of the race and set the fastest lap, just for something to do.' If ever there was an indictment of the inability of cars to run in close company in 2007 then, Räikkönen's typical insouciance notwithstanding, this was it.

Massa's victory meant that all four of the championship contenders had each scored three wins. The spread of points had narrowed from 21 to 16. There were five races to go and everything to play for within each team. The question was, would McLaren and Ferrari consider taking the painful decision to favour one driver over another?

19

Same Old, Same Old

The place may be old and frayed at its edges but, for that very reason, the Autodromo di Monza has an attraction as enduring as the sound of its name when rattled off in a fanatical Italian tongue. The expression 'theatre of motor sport' is bandied about but nowhere comes close to Monza when embracing all that is dramatic and passionate about motor racing. The ancient park, in the northern suburbs of Milan, is redolent with memories, some thrilling, others desperately sad. You are reminded of them instantly from the moment you drive through the gates and take in an atmosphere that has no equal.

Monza has been the home of the Italian Grand Prix for more than eighty years. During that time, legends have grown, heroes have come and gone; but the place remains essentially the same since the day the Italian motor industry felt it should have a permanent and enclosed racing circuit. Legend has it that 3000 men took 110 days in 1922 to complete a 6.21-mile combination of road circuit and banked track in a park adjoining the royal villa not far from the centre of Monza.

Although the banked section has long since been abandoned, the towering concrete edifice remains as a memorial to speed, which is the very essence of Monza. When Peter Gethin led four cars, running almost side-by-side, across the line in 1971, the British driver's winning average in excess of 150 m.p.h. struck fear into the hearts of the authorities. Monza was flat out, more or less from the start to the finish of the lap. The subsequent inclusion of chicanes may have brought the necessary reduction in speed but they did not remove the unique atmosphere of a track running through a tree-lined park. Throw in a traditional date in early September and the picture is completed by a warm, still day with its dappled sunlight. All seems well with the world.

Except that, usually, it is not. An exciting undercurrent of barely controlled chaos seems to pervade the atmosphere from the moment the teams arrive to do business. In 2006, the FIA stewards reached one of their most bizarre decisions ever following an incident during qualifying for the Grand Prix.

Fernando Alonso, then driving for Renault, had suffered a sudden loss of pressure in his right-rear tyre. Subsequent examination by Michelin showed that something had punctured the tread, leaving a sizeable hole. Unfortunately, the tyre had collapsed at the start of a lap, leaving Alonso to motor as quickly as he could for 3 miles before reaching the pits. The Renault team found that the flailing rubber had done significant damage to the car's rear sidepod, badly affecting the aerodynamics and downforce. There was no time for anything other than a change of tyre as qualifying was into its final minutes.

Alonso was sent on his way in the knowledge that the rear of the car was damaged – but he did not know by how much. He did, however, know that he had to go flat out if he was to cross the line and start what would be his last qualifying lap before the chequered flag appeared. He made it with 2 seconds to go.

His lap was worth fifth on the grid; a phenomenal effort considering the commitment necessary with a damaged car on a track where 200 m.p.h. is the terminal speed in three places. But, while that seemed to be the end of Alonso's dramas, it was, in fact, only the beginning.

When Alonso had left the pits and accelerated towards the first chicane, Massa was about to start his final flying lap. The

Ferrari driver later claimed he had been impeded by Alonso, otherwise he would have had pole position rather than fourth fastest time. The race stewards, on examining the evidence, found in Massa's favour and stripped Alonso of his three fastest lap times, thus demoting the world champion from fifth to tenth on the grid. Renault, Alonso and, it has to be said, about 99 per cent of the paddock were stunned.

The stewards accepted that Alonso had been flat out in order to beat the chequered flag. But, they claimed, the evidence showed that Massa had been quicker than the Renault through the final sector of the lap. Which indeed he had – thanks to receiving a tow from the Renault by slip-streaming on the back straight.

Massa then claimed that the understeer (the car wanting to go straight on rather than turn) experienced at the final corner had been induced by the dirty air from the Renault – a fact that was difficult to credit because Massa's on-car video showed Alonso to be several car lengths ahead. As the Renault engineers were to later point out, they had proof that their drivers had experienced similar understeer problems when running alone and thanks to arriving too quickly and placing excessive load on the front-left tyre. The officials, however, contended that a driver on an 'out' lap must give way to a driver on a flying lap. Massa, they said, was the innocent party and had been penalized unfairly.

This prompted Alonso to say he loved the spirit of motor racing but felt that F1 was no longer a sport, a view which Max Mosley tritely dismissed as being 'understandably emotional'. Mosley may have been technically correct in everything he said but he was inviting hostile reaction from critics who felt that, not for the first time in 2006, Renault's championship campaign was being compromised. At best, the FIA's ruling and its timing could be described as unfortunate.

Flavio Briatore, the boss of Renault, was furious, claiming the championship was being settled 'around a table rather than on the track'. He later rescinded his remarks due, it is believed, to a threat to be charged for bringing the sport into disrepute.

Mosley said Massa had been the innocent party and had been unfairly penalized because the Ferrari had been disturbed by the back draught from the Renault. This was a dubious contention thanks to the distance between the two cars and Alonso's speed as he raced to beat the clock. Mosley then side-stepped that question by telling BBC Radio 5 Live that he always accepted the decisions of the stewards, a curious comment which immediately invited several listeners to remind Mosley of an incident earlier in the year when the FIA had taken its own stewards to court after a decision reached (in favour of Renault) over the legality of Alonso's car in Germany.

Mosley's reputation came under further close examination by Martin Brundle during the ITV commentator's walk on the starting grid at Monza. Mosley, clearly on the back foot, chose to question Brundle's qualification to comment on the juxtaposition of the two cars. This was another strange remark offered, this time, to a driver who had seen the evidence and who had competed in more than 150 Grands Prix, unlike most FIA stewards whose experience of fast motoring was likely to have been limited to the back of a chauffeur-driven car on its way to an expensive dinner. It would not be the last time Mosley and Brundle would have their disagreements in public.

Whatever the rights and wrongs, the stewards' decision was final. The unfortunate aspect of this case was that it involved a Renault and a Ferrari, thus triggering the predictable claim that the FIA was trying to nobble Renault in favour of Ferrari, a fanciful suggestion at the time but one that would gather currency a year later as the McLaren and Ferrari spy case continued to unravel, seemingly in Ferrari's favour.

The animosity between Ferrari and McLaren stretched back to 1976, another year when they were neck-and-neck in the championship. And, once again, the actions of officials at Monza had heightened the tension, not that it was necessary during a season of drama and emotion. The title, being fought between Niki Lauda and James Hunt, appeared to be over when Lauda was severely burned and given the last rites after crashing during the German Grand Prix.

Six weeks later, his head heavily bandaged, Lauda made a dramatic return to the Ferrari cockpit – at Monza, of all places. The effect on the ardent Ferrari fans can be imagined. In the meantime, Hunt had reduced Lauda's championship lead to just 2 points and here he was on the front row at Monza. But not for long. The authorities, claiming Hunt's McLaren was using illegal fuel, demoted the Englishman to the back of the grid. Hunt retired and Lauda finished a remarkable fourth. Game on. All was well with the world at Monza.

McLaren were to have more problems with officials at Monza ten years later. The long straights had, once again, played into the hands of the powerful BMW turbos, Teo Fabi touching 214 m.p.h. during qualifying as the Italian put his Benetton on pole. Prost was alongside in his McLaren. Or, at least, he should have been. In one of the most unusual starts seen before or since, the 1986 Italian Grand Prix would get under way minus the entire front row of the grid.

Fabi stalled his BMW engine just as the field was flagged off on the final parade lap. Prost, meanwhile, was going nowhere, a faulty alternator preventing the TAG-Porsche V6 from starting. Prost sprang from the car and ran to the end of the pit lane, where the spare McLaren was waiting. (Such a late swap was permitted then, but no longer in 2007.) Prost joined in as soon as the twenty-six cars had left the grid at the start. Really fired up, the Frenchman was into tenth place in as many laps. He got as far as fifth before making a scheduled pit stop on lap 22, rejoining in ninth place and preparing to continue his quest for championship points. Meanwhile, in the race control office . . .

The stewards had been in session since the beginning of the

179

race. It took this august body 26 laps, or the best part of 40 minutes, to decide that Prost should not have been allowed to start. The rules said that a driver could not change cars once the green flag had been waved to signal the start of the parade lap. It had been plain to everyone, except the stewards it seemed, that Prost had made the switch after the appearance of the green flag and yet he had been allowed to not only start but also to drive the wheels off the McLaren for 26 highly impressive laps. In fact, it would have come to nothing in any case since Prost's engine expired just after he had been signalled to stop. But that did not detract from a serious case of fumbling by the officials.

Prost joined Senna on the retirement list, the Lotus driver having stopped with a broken clutch on the first lap. All of which was good news for Williams as Piquet and Mansell moved forward to score a one–two, Mansell being unable to match his team-mate and recognizing the fact by graciously pulling alongside and applauding Piquet on the slowing-down lap. Mansell now had 61 points, Piquet 56 and Prost 53. Senna, on 48, was gradually slipping out of the equation. The betting was on one of the Williams drivers; Prost was considered the outsider. At the time, this seemed unbearably tense. But it was to be child's play when compared with the seething discontent at Monza twenty-one years later.

20
Tit for Tedious Tat

By the time the teams reached Monza in 2007, the championship seemed a minor consideration as the politics notched up several more gears. One effect of the discord within McLaren in Hungary had been to remove attention from the ongoing argument with Ferrari. Everything had seemed settled following the verdict of the World Motor Sport Council in favour of McLaren on 26 July. A few days later, Max Mosley received a letter from Luigi Macaluso, president of the Italian motoring authority, the ACI-CSAI.

Dear President,
We have been informed about the outcome of the most recent meeting of the World Motor Sport Council held on July 26, 2007 in Paris. We have also exchanged views with our licence holder, Scuderia Ferrari Marlboro (owned by Ferrari SpA).

We must confess that we find it quite difficult to justify how a team has not been penalised while it has been found in breach of clause 151c of the International Sporting Code. Indeed, this is probably the most fundamental provision of our sport.

In the present case the infringement is very serious since it has been assessed that the team Vodafone McLaren Mercedes has repeatedly breached such provision, over several months, through several top team representatives, to the detriment of its most direct competitor and therefore to its direct or indirect advantage and knowing that such infringement would still be ongoing had it not been fortuitously discovered.

The very fact that the breach of clause 151c has been assessed by the World Motor Sport Council means that all conditions of such breach were fulfilled. We cannot see why additional conditions would have to be demonstrated in order for a penalty to be inflicted.

The recent history of Formula One offers several examples of cases in which a party was inflicted a severe penalty because of a breach of clause 151c, without the subject matter of such breach having been used by a team or having had any effect on the outcome of the competition.

We fear that the decision of the World Motor Sport Council could create a precedent which, at this level of the sport and stage of the competition, would be highly inappropriate and detrimental for the sport.

In any event, in view of the aforesaid, we respectfully suggest that you, in your capacity as President of the FIA, in accordance with the powers granted to you by clause 23 paragraph 1 of the FIA Statutes and article 1 of the CIA rules, submit the matter to the International Court of Appeal of the FIA.

This would also enable our licence holder, Ferrari, on behalf of which we would take part in the proceedings, and perhaps other teams as well, to fully submit their position and protect their rights. In effect, Ferrari – as at least two other teams – attended the World Motor Sport Council in Paris as observers and not as a party.

Accordingly, they did not have a full right of audience. As, however, Ferrari in any event had been seriously and

directly affected by McLaren's behaviour, we deem it
appropriate that Ferrari (directly or through ourselves)
enjoys full rights of due process which would be the case
in accordance with the rules applicable in front of the
International Court of Appeal.

Yours sincerely

Luigi Macaluso

The President of ACI-CSAI

Copy to: Ferrari SpA, Maranello, Att. Jean Todt, CEO

The FIA chose to refer Ferrari's complaint to a court of appeal.
McLaren responded with a press release:

Following a thoroughly misleading press campaign by
Ferrari and pressure from the Automobile Club D'Italia, the
FIA has asked the FIA International Court of Appeal to con-
sider the unanimous decision made by the World Motor
Sport Council on 26th July 2007.

Having considered in great detail the full submissions of
both Ferrari and McLaren, the World Motor Sport Council
determined that there was no evidence that any information, passed by a Ferrari team member to a McLaren
employee, had been brought into the organisation or provided any benefit whatsoever to the McLaren programme.

McLaren is not aware of any new information or arguments that have arisen since the meeting of the World Motor
Sport Council and therefore assumes that these same mate-
rials will now be considered by the FIA International Court
of Appeal.

Whilst this is both disappointing and time-consuming,
McLaren is confident that the FIA International Court of
Appeal will also exonerate McLaren and we will in the
meanwhile continue to focus on our current World
Championship programme.

When the Ferrari board of directors met and supported the decision to appeal against the decision to clear Ferrari, Dennis constructed a lengthy letter to Macaluso.

1 August 2007

Dear Mr Macaluso,

ARTICLE 151C OF THE INTERNATIONAL SPORTING CODE

I refer to your letter dated 30 July 2007 to Mr Mosley of the FIA and to Mr Mosley's reply to you dated 31 July 2007, both of which were published on the FIA website yesterday without McLaren being given any opportunity at all to comment on this exchange of letters.

In your letter to the FIA you state that you *find it quite difficult to justify how a team has not been penalised while it has been found in breach of clause 151c of the International Sporting Code.*

As it is apparent from your letter that you have only heard Ferrari's version of events, I would like to set the record straight and to explain to you in some detail why it was entirely fair that McLaren was not penalised and why it would in fact also have been fair if McLaren had not been found to be in breach of Article 151c at all.

Since this matter first came to light, McLaren has been completely open with Ferrari and the FIA and has cooperated to the fullest extent in the investigation of the facts.

At the hearing before the World Motor Sport Council, I and senior members of McLaren's staff gave evidence and were cross-examined by the Council and by Ferrari. We presented to the Council and to Ferrari all of McLaren's relevant documentary records for consideration. All of this evidence was fully tested at the hearing.

Our evidence makes it completely clear that the true facts of this matter are as follows:

'Whistle-blowing' in March 2007

In March 2007, Mr Stepney of Ferrari contacted Mr Coughlan and informed him about two aspects of the Ferrari car which he regarded being in breach of FIA regulations. Specifically, he told Mr Coughlan about a floor attachment mechanism and a rear wing separator, both of which could be and were seen on the Ferrari car prior to the Australian Grand Prix.

Mr Coughlan immediately told McLaren's senior management about Mr Stepney's allegations. McLaren took steps to confirm whether the allegations were true, and we concluded that they were. Accordingly we reported these two matters to the FIA, adopting the customary practice of asking the FIA Technical Department for their opinion.

As regards the rear wing separator, the FIA subsequently ruled that this was compliant with the Technical Regulations. However the FIA ruled that this floor device was illegal. You will appreciate the significance of this.

As far as we are aware, Ferrari ran their cars with this illegal device at the Australian Grand Prix, which they won. In the interests of the sport, McLaren chose not to protest the result of the Australian Grand Prix even though it seems clear that Ferrari had an illegal competitive advantage.

Ferrari only withdrew the floor device after it was confirmed to be illegal by the FIA. Were it not for Mr Stepney drawing this illegal device to the attention of McLaren, and McLaren drawing it to the attention of the FIA, there is every reason to suppose that Ferrari would have continued to race with an illegal car.

Chequered Conflict

In the press, Ferrari have described the information which Mr Stepney provided to Mr Coughlan in March 2007 as being Ferrari's 'confidential information'. This is completely misleading. There is nothing confidential about the rear wing separator, which is immediately visible on the exterior of the car.

As regards the floor device, Mr Stepney revealed that Ferrari was proposing to use an illegal device at the Australian Grand Prix and no doubt for the rest of the season. He acted properly and in the interests of the sport in 'blowing the whistle' about this. No team can expect their employees to keep quiet if they suspect – correctly in this case – that their employers are breaching the rules of the sport.

Ferrari have also complained in the press that McLaren and I in particular should have disclosed to Ferrari that it was Mr Stepney who blew the whistle on their illegal floor device. They also criticise me for entering a gentlemen's agreement in April 2007 about how to conduct technical complaints without revealing that it was Mr Stepney who made the disclosures in March.

For reasons which must be obvious to anyone fair minded, I reject these criticisms absolutely. I did not think it correct to disclose the name of the whistle-blower to Ferrari as it is not in the interests of Formula 1 for members of teams to feel that they cannot disclose instances of illegal activity without risking their name being disclosed to their employer. It is in the interests of Formula 1 that whistle-blowing is encouraged and not discouraged. If team members think that their identity will be revealed they will not whistle-blow.

What McLaren did do was to take steps immediately after learning of the contact between Mr Stepney and Mr Coughlan in March 2007 to ensure that Mr Stepney and Mr Coughlan ceased having any contact.

Whilst we saw nothing wrong with Mr Stepney
whistle-blowing on Ferrari's illegal activities, we felt that it
was not helpful for him to choose Mr Coughlan to blow
the whistle to. We did not feel comfortable with a
disgruntled Mr Stepney being in contact with Mr
Coughlan. For this reason in March 2007, immediately
after the Australian Grand Prix, Mr Coughlan was
instructed by his superior Mr Neale to cease contact with
Mr Stepney.

In summary, faced with clear information that Ferrari
was proposing to use an illegal device, McLaren acted
entirely properly, indeed we acted with considerable
restraint. If any criticism is to be made, then I suggest that
you should reflect carefully on the conduct of your licence
holder, Ferrari, which appears to have won the Australian
Grand Prix by racing with an illegal device.

The 'Ferrari Documents'

I turn now to the events which occurred later in the year
between Mr Stepney and Mr Coughlan and in particular to
the provision of a 'dossier' of Ferrari Documents by Mr
Stepney to Mr Coughlan at a meeting in Barcelona on
Saturday 28 April 2007.

As I will explain, these events are quite separate from
Mr Stepney's whistle-blowing in March 2007, because
during this period Mr Coughlan was acting secretly, in
breach of his contract with McLaren, and for his own
private purposes, quite conceivably as part of a scheme to
leave McLaren and join another team together with Mr
Stepney.

The background to the meeting on Saturday 28 April
2007 is set out in correspondence from Ron Dennis which
claims that in early April 2007, Mr Coughlan told Mr
Neale that despite his best efforts to cut off contact, Mr

Stepney continued to contact him to express grievances about his lot with Ferrari. Mr Neale arranged for the installation of a 'firewall' on McLaren's computer system to stop emails from Mr Stepney.

In addition to this Mr Coughlan said to Mr Neale that the only way he thought that this would stop is if Mr Coughlan spoke to Mr Stepney face to face and told him to stop trying to contact him. Mr Neale agreed that he could do this outside working hours.

On Saturday 28 April 2007, Mr Coughlan went to Barcelona and met Mr Stepney. Only Mr Coughlan and Mr Stepney know what truly happened at that meeting. So far as McLaren was concerned, however, when Mr Coughlan returned to work, he told Mr Neale that his meeting with Mr Stepney had achieved its objective and he believed that Mr Stepney would not contact him again.

After this, no-one at McLaren heard anything more about contact between Mr Stepney and Mr Coughlan until 3 July 2007. Everyone at McLaren assumed that the issue of Mr Stepney contacting Mr Coughlan to express grievances had been resolved.

On 3 July 2007, Ferrari executed a search order at Mr Coughlan's home and seized two CDs containing Ferrari Documents. I emphasise that these documents were found at Mr Coughlan's home. No Ferrari Documents were found at McLaren's offices.

As is now in the public domain, Mr Coughlan has admitted that Mr Stepney gave him a dossier of Ferrari Documents in Barcelona which he took for his own private reasons, he says 'engineering curiosity'.

He kept these Documents at his home, and later with the assistance of his wife copied onto two CDs at a shop near their home, before shredding the originals using a home shredder and burning them in his back garden. Mr

Coughlan says that he made no use of the Documents at work and that no one else at McLaren knew that he had taken the Documents.

Since Ferrari discovered that Mr Coughlan had the Ferrari Documents at his home, it has gone to extraordinary lengths to try to maximise the damage to McLaren, no doubt hoping to gain some advantage for the World Championship.

In particular, Ferrari has alleged, without any justification, that other McLaren staff were aware of what Mr Coughlan had done and that McLaren made some use of the Documents. Ferrari has no evidence whatsoever for these offensive and false allegations and presented no such evidence to the World Motor Sports Council. The Council quite correctly rejected these allegations.

As regards Ferrari's allegation that other McLaren staff were aware of what Mr Coughlan had done, in its statements to the press, Ferrari has tried to confuse the March 2007 whistle-blowing by Mr Stepney (which McLaren did know about) with the events on and following 28 April 2007 (which Mr Coughlan kept completely secret).

Let me make it clear: McLaren did know about the whistle-blowing matters in March 2007 – indeed it reported these matters to the FIA. However that has nothing to do with what Mr Coughlan did on and after 28 April 2007. McLaren management and staff had no knowledge whatsoever about that.

In addition to this, Ferrari has tried to latch on to two instances where Mr Coughlan has stated that he showed single pages which he says were from the Ferrari Documents to two other McLaren staff: Mr Taylor (another McLaren engineer who had previously worked with Mr Coughlan when they were both at Ferrari) and Mr Neale (Mr Coughlan's superior).

The Council has fully investigated these instances, and concluded quite rightly that neither Mr Taylor nor Mr Neale were aware that the single pages they were shown were Ferrari confidential information, still less that they were part of a dossier of several hundred pages which Mr Coughlan had secretly received and kept at his house.

So far as Mr Taylor is concerned, Mr Coughlan briefly showed him a single diagram. Mr Taylor had no idea whether this was an old or new diagram and had no idea it came from Mr Stepney. He was not given a copy and made no use of the diagram. He paid no attention to the incident.

As for Mr Neale, he had an informal meeting at a restaurant on 25 May 2007 to discuss a request Mr Coughlan had made for an early release from his contract of employment with McLaren.

Towards the end of this Mr Coughlan began to show Mr Neale two images, but Mr Neale stated that he was not interested in seeing them. Mr Neale has stated that these images did not appear to have any connection with Ferrari or any other team. When asked at the hearing about this, Mr Neale said that although this was only speculation on his part, he thought that Mr Coughlan was about to refer to the images to seek resources from him for digital mock up equipment.

In short these instances did not alert Mr Taylor or Mr Neale that Mr Coughlan had taken possession of the Ferrari Documents. Neither they or any other member of McLaren staff had any idea what Mr Coughlan had done.

I turn then to Ferrari's allegation that McLaren somehow made use of the Ferrari Documents which Mr Coughlan kept secretly at his home.

Mr Coughlan himself is categoric that he made no use of the Ferrari Documents in the McLaren car. Mr

Coughlan's job related to the management of drawing production by the design staff and their sign off prior to issue to our production facilities. He did not have responsibility for the performance enhancement of the car.

This function lies with the Chief Engineers and R&D Team who report to the Engineering Director, Patrick Lowe, who provided detailed evidence to the World Motor Sport Council. An important part of Mr Coughlan's job was, however, monitoring the testing and reliability of the car throughout the year.

In addition to this functional analysis, McLaren had conducted a very thorough physical and electronic search (conducted by Kroll) and a thorough engineering study conducted by Patrick Lowe to see if any of the Ferrari Documents were or are at McLaren or if any use of such documents has actually been made in relation to the McLaren car.

This investigation has confirmed that none of the Ferrari Documents were at McLaren as opposed to at Mr Coughlan's home and that there is no possibility that any of the information in those Documents could have been used on any development on the McLaren car.

At the hearing, McLaren demonstrated clearly to the satisfaction of the World Motor Sport Council that no use whatsoever has been made of any of the contents of the Ferrari Documents in the McLaren car.

Accordingly, Ferrari's continued allegations in the press that McLaren has made use of the Ferrari Documents are entirely false.

I deal lastly with Mr Coughlan's true motives for taking and keeping the Ferrari Documents. Although McLaren cannot know for sure what Mr Coughlan's (and Mr Stepney's) motives were, what McLaren do know is that only a few days after the 28 April Mr Stepney contacted

Honda (on 2 May) and commenced a process whereby Mr Stepney and Mr Coughlan together offered their services to join Honda. McLaren believes that it is highly likely that Mr Stepney provided the Ferrari Documents to Mr Coughlan as part of a joint scheme to seek employment at another team.

These are the facts. Although McLaren does not know for sure what Mr Stepney's purpose was in passing the Ferrari Documents to Mr Coughlan and what Mr Coughlan's purpose was in receiving them, McLaren does know for sure that Mr Coughlan acted secretly and that the Ferrari Documents were not used in the McLaren car but that Mr Stepney and Mr Coughlan were looking to leaving Ferrari and McLaren to join another team.

It is fact that Mr Coughlan never passed the Ferrari Documents to anyone else at McLaren or told anyone at McLaren that he had these documents. It is fact that no-one at McLaren knew that Mr Coughlan had received any Documents from Mr Stepney on the 28 April. It is fact that Mr Coughlan had been told by his superior Mr Neale to stop all contact with Mr Stepney straight after the Australian Grand Prix.

Other matters

Your letter also suggests that the outcome might have been different if the Council had given Ferrari further opportunities to be heard beyond those offered. I again ask you to look at the real facts, which are that Ferrari fully participated in the hearing before the Council.

First, Ferrari submitted a lengthy, albeit grossly misleading, memorandum dated 16 July 2007 along with supporting documents which together totalled 118 pages.

Ferrari did not send McLaren the memorandum. The memorandum was circulated to the Council on the 20 July.

McLaren did not see it until two days before the hearing
and it was only then that we were able to correct its
grossly inaccurate contents.

In the meantime, the misleading Ferrari memorandum
or sections of it appear to have been leaked to the Italian
press as much of the Italian press reports echo elements of
that memorandum.

In addition to this Ferrari, who were represented by
lawyers, were given several opportunities by the FIA
President to ask questions and make submissions
throughout the hearing. Mr Todt also gave evidence.

It was clear that the FIA President afforded Ferrari
every opportunity to be heard in order to ensure that all
relevant matters were heard by the WMSC. Indeed, at the
very end of the proceeding, Ferrari intervened with a
request to make further closing comments. Ferrari's
request was permitted and their lawyer proceeded to
make further detailed closing comments at some length.

I therefore simply do not understand what basis there is
for Ferrari's claim that it was denied an opportunity to put
its case. It put its case both in writing and orally.

I respectfully ask you and the ACI-CSAI to look at the
hard facts of this matter in an objective and fair manner
rather than being influenced by selective and misleading
statements put out with the object of damaging McLaren.

The reason McLaren was not penalised is that the
World Motor Sport Council rightly concluded that it
should not be blamed for Mr Coughlan's actions. It based
its decision on solid facts and not false innuendo.
McLaren's reputation has been unfairly sullied by
incorrect press reports from Italy and grossly misleading
statements from Ferrari.

This is a fantastic World Championship and it would be
a tragedy if one of the best World Championships in years

was derailed by the acts of one Ferrari and one McLaren employee acting for their own purposes wholly unconnected with Ferrari or McLaren.

We believe that the Ferrari press releases, the leaks to the Italian press and recent events have been damaging to Formula 1 as well as McLaren. The World Championship should be contested on the track not in Courts or in the press.

We will naturally present our case before the FIA Court of Appeal as we strongly believe McLaren has done nothing wrong. It is our belief that justice will prevail and that McLaren will not be penalised.

Yours sincerely,

Ron Dennis CBE

Group Chairman and CEO

Copy: Max Mosley, President FIA; Jean Todt, CEO Ferrari SpA

Macaluso issued a succinct reply the following day.

2 August 2007

Dear Mr Dennis,

Article 151c of the International Sporting Code

I refer to your letter of 1 August 2007.

It is apparent from your letter that there is a distinct difference between McLaren's view of events and that of Ferrari. It therefore seems appropriate for the matter to be reviewed by the International Court of Appeal as decided by the FIA President, Mr Mosley.

It is not my role nor would it be appropriate for me to answer your various points. It will be for the Court of Appeal to do so.

In any event, I would limit myself to stress that McLaren was found in breach of Article 151c of the

International Sporting Code, but nevertheless escaped any penalty.

As Mr Mosley indicated in his letter of 31 July 2007, it is important for the World Championship that the correct outcome is reached. It is clearly in the interest of the sport that the appropriate precedent for dealing with events such as these is set.

At the hearing of the World Motor Sport Council on 26 July 2007, Ferrari was legally represented but attended the meeting merely as an observer.

It accordingly did not have sufficient opportunity to present to the Council or ask questions of key individuals involved in this matter in order to test their evidence.

A hearing before the International Court of Appeal will allow Ferrari an opportunity to present its evidence and arguments in detail.

Yours sincerely

Luigi Macaluso

The President of ACI-CSAI

Copy: Mr Max Mosley (President FIA); Mr Jean Todt (CEO Ferrari SpA)

One response then followed another, the content of the letters becoming more trivial and tedious by the day. There were two minor but interesting points of note: one, Ferrari and anyone associated with the Italian team did not waste a single oppor- tunity to mention and thereby embarrass Vodafone, the telecommunications company that had become McLaren's title sponsor after leaving Ferrari, where there had been no opportu- nity for similar exposure thanks to Marlboro's dominance. And two, Mr Macaluso was president of Girard-Perregaux, the com- pany that made expensive wristwatches under licence for Ferrari. While this had no bearing whatsoever on the handling of Macaluso's duties in connection with the Ferrari spy scandal, the link between the two caused a number of eyebrows to be raised within the cynical world of F1.

The affair took on a more serious tone a few weeks later when the FIA scrapped the appeal hearing and announced plans to reconvene the World Motor Sport Council on 13 September because important new evidence had become known. This involved the emails between the McLaren drivers that were alleged to demonstrate that McLaren officials knew more about the Ferrari information than they were letting on. Clearly, this matter, with assistance from Ferrari and the FIA, was going to run and run. Ultimately, and despite the lofty and misguided pleas of innocence from Dennis in the letters above, the FIA would have good cause. Unfortunately, the governing body's manner of handling it would throw more fat on a fire that was becoming a raging inferno.

21
Winning Where it Matters

The hostility between Ferrari and McLaren was palpable. The tension at Monza was not eased when the Italian police arrived in the paddock to notify four McLaren officials that they were to be the subject of a civil inquiry. This was not news to McLaren since the serving of such notices was a matter of legal routine but the police presence – seized upon by photographers who had been mysteriously tipped off – merely twisted the knife once more in McLaren's corporate underbelly.

The last thing McLaren needed was to have headlines such as the one in the *Sunday Times* stating 'Police Swoop on McLaren'. That would have been funny were it not such a serious subject. The police officers had been greeted on arrival at the McLaren Brand Centre by Justine Blake, PA to Ron Dennis. They had quietly and politely explained the purpose of their visit and Ms Blake duly noted the facts officially before showing the officers around the impressive facility. The beaming officials then emerged, each clutching a goody bag and a McLaren cap. Hardly a police swoop, but a development that was indicative of the pressure being applied.

Later that afternoon, Dennis had his usual briefing with the media. He was asked if this had been the worst experience in his twenty-five years in F1.

'It's certainly the most extreme I've been through,' said

Dennis. 'I think that's apparent to everybody.' When asked if he was contemplating standing down, Dennis said he had considered it but rejected the idea as this was not the right moment. 'With regard to the bigger issues, I'm doing the best job I can of addressing them, working hard, putting lots of hours in,' he said. 'But it's not great, is it? Sometimes I get a bit confused by many things in life and this one's pretty confusing.'

The bitterness between Ferrari and McLaren accentuated the need for action on the track to speak louder than some of the questionable statements issuing from all sides in a quarrel that had been inflated far beyond the original sin of a Ferrari employee foolishly leaking information and a McLaren engineer receiving and keeping it.

For 82 seconds during Saturday's qualifying at Monza, Alonso put the politics of F1 behind him to not only beat Ferrari but also to lay down a marker for Hamilton as the McLaren drivers fought over pole position for the Italian Grand Prix. Having established that he had the legs of the Ferrari drivers to the tune of half a second a lap, an exceptional margin by recent standards, Alonso focused on a lap that clearly gave Hamilton food for thought as he studied the times after stepping from his car.

This in-house battle was played out before an unusually quiet audience as the normally vociferous fans, the 'tifosi', attempted, with obvious difficulty, to swallow the news that the enemy had arrived on their doorstep and given the home team a pasting. Massa claimed third fastest time but Ferrari's cause had not been helped during the morning's free practice when Räikkönen had crashed heavily. The Finn lost control on one of the many bumps that characterize the elderly race track and he was lucky to escape unhurt after going headlong into a tyre barrier at over 100 m.p.h.

Räikkönen switched to the spare Ferrari but avoided a ten-place grid penalty for using a different engine thanks to the team switching the V8 from his crashed car. Räikkönen had no time in which to fine-tune the new chassis and he received another setback when Heidfeld's BMW demoted the Ferrari to fifth place during the last lap of qualifying.

The majority of F1 insiders wanted to see McLaren win for reasons that went beyond humbling Ferrari. Dennis may not have been the most popular man in the paddock yet it was an indication of the unease over his perceived ill-treatment by Ferrari and the FIA that a victory for McLaren on the racetrack would at least bring satisfaction where it ought to matter most.

McLaren were expending money and manpower on their legal defence, a serious distraction that doubtless pleased Ferrari as the championship headed towards its conclusion. Meanwhile, the FIA denied suggestions that this was nothing more than a witch-hunt and an extension of what was widely considered to be a simmering animosity between Mosley and Dennis. An FIA spokesman said:

This inquiry was triggered by a letter of complaint from Ferrari which was, in turn, triggered by the extraordinary discovery of 780 pages of their most confidential technical information in the hands of McLaren's chief designer. Under the circumstances, the suggestion that the FIA's ongoing investigation is about anything other than the pursuit of sporting fairness demonstrates a blinding refusal to accept the basic facts.

Such a robust defence refuted the rumour that leading F1 figures had suggested to Dennis that if he resigned, matters could be brought to an immediate close. Dennis made it clear that he had no intention of doing so and turned his attention to the race at Monza.

Chequered Conflict

Hamilton made a slow start from the dirty side of the front row and was overtaken by Massa. But, showing the same aggressive form seen at the first corner in Australia, Hamilton ran round the outside, taking the place back from Massa and almost overtaking Alonso's leading car in the process. Massa launched a strong attack but Hamilton managed to hold him off. That would be the last of Massa's efforts. A few laps later, he was in the pits complaining of difficult handling due, he thought, to a rear puncture. A return to the track with fresh rubber merely confirmed that the problem remained. Massa was retired with what Ferrari described as mechanical problems with the rear of the car. The media was left to speculate whether or not Räikkönen's crash – allegedly caused by a bump on the track – had been linked to a similar problem.

Räikkönen, meanwhile, hung on to the McLarens as best he could, a one-stop strategy appearing to work for the Ferrari driver when he jumped ahead of Hamilton as the Englishman made his second stop. But that did not take into account Hamilton's aggressive state of mind as he thought more about Alonso's leading McLaren than the Ferrari ahead of him. In a move that clearly caught Räikkönen by surprise, Hamilton came from a long way back to out-brake the Ferrari into the first chicane, smoke pouring off Hamilton's right-front tyre. As far as the Ferrari fans were concerned, this was the final insult. A McLaren one–two was more than they could take and the grandstands began to empty.

The post-race issue of *The Red Bulletin*, miraculously produced within hours of the finish, summed up the mood. The cover, with the headline 'Hunting Hamilton', portrayed Alonso spraying champagne. Inside, a full-page photo showed an exhausted Ron Dennis holding back the tears, watched by his concerned press officer, Ellen Kolby. A one–two victory had been the perfect riposte but, after a weekend of tension, it was almost too much for Dennis to take. If he thought that was bad, then worse was to follow in the coming week. Meanwhile, another dramatic Italian Grand Prix, theatrical even by Monza's standards, was done.

22

McLaren Laid Bare

The World Motor Sport Council met in Paris on the Thursday preceding the Belgian Grand Prix. After an all-day sitting and powerful legal arguments from all sides, the council found that McLaren were not guilty of incorporating Ferrari's details in their car, the MP4/22. But it was agreed that possession of the information had bestowed McLaren with a 'significant sporting advantage'. For this, McLaren were stripped of their team championship points and fined $100 million, a record amount for any indiscretion, never mind a charge characterized by phrases such as 'insufficient evidence', 'impossible to quantify' and 'some degree of advantage was confirmed'.

The day-long session revealed that, during the first three races in March and April, Alonso and Pedro de la Rosa had been aware of information concerning the technical set-up of the 2007 Ferrari and its operation. Coughlan had supplied these details from conversations and SMS texts with Stepney. In a fourteen-page document, the FIA detailed how the World Motor Sport Council reached its verdict.

In the emails, de la Rosa talked about information coming from Stepney. On 21 March de la Rosa wrote to Coughlan: *Hi Mike, do you know the Red Car's Weight Distribution? It would be important for us to know so that we could try it in the simulator. Thanks in advance, Pedro. P.S. I will be in the simulator tomorrow.*

Chequered Conflict

Coughlan replied with a text message, giving the required details although, in the end, those settings were not tried.

On 25 March, de la Rosa sent an email to Alonso setting out the weight distribution to two decimal places on each of Ferrari's cars for the Australian Grand Prix. Alonso then replied: *Its [the Ferrari's] weight distribution surprises me; I don't know either if it's 100 percent reliable, but at least it draws attention.*

De la Rosa replied: *All the information from Ferrari is very reliable. It comes from Nigel Stepney, their former chief mechanic – I don't know what post he holds now. He's the same person who told us in Australia that Kimi was stopping in lap 18. He's very friendly with Mike Coughlan, our Chief Designer, and he told him that.*

The evidence then detailed emails from de la Rosa discussing a flexible wing, aero balance, tyre gas, Ferrari's braking system and the team's stopping strategy. The FIA also examined reports from the Italian police illustrating call logs between Coughlan and Stepney. The evidence said: 'In total, at least 288 SMS messages and 35 telephone calls appear to have passed between Coughlan and Stepney between 11 March 2007 and 3 July 2007.'

The World Motor Sport Council found that:

- Coughlan had more information than previously appreciated and was receiving information in a systematic manner over a period of months;
- the information has been disseminated, at least to some degree (e.g. to Mr. De la Rosa and Mr. Alonso), within the McLaren team;
- the information being disseminated within the McLaren team included not only highly sensitive technical information but also secret information regarding Ferrari's sporting strategy;
- Mr. de la Rosa, in the performance of his functions at McLaren, requested and received secret Ferrari information from a source which he knew to be illegitimate

and expressly stated that the purpose of his request was to run tests in the simulator;
- the secret information in question was shared with Mr. Alonso;
- there was a clear intention on the part of a number of McLaren personnel to use some of the Ferrari confidential information in its own testing. If this was not in fact carried into effect it was only because there were technical reasons not to do so;
- Coughlan's role within McLaren (as now understood by the WMSC) put him in a position in which his knowledge of the secret Ferrari information would have influenced him in the performance of his duties.

This seemed a damning conclusion until the statement said the following: 'The WMSC does not have evidence that any complete Ferrari design was copied and subsequently wholly incorporated into the McLaren car as a result of Coughlan passing confidential information from Stepney to McLaren. However, it is difficult to accept that the secret Ferrari information that was within Coughlan's knowledge never influenced his judgement in the performance of his duties.' The statement added: 'The WMSC believes that the nature of the information illicitly held by McLaren was information of a nature which, if used or in any way taken into account, could confer a significant sporting advantage upon McLaren.'

In essence, the hearing revealed that Dennis, admired for his management skills, actually knew less about what was going on within his team than he thought he did. This was just as damaging as the public exposure of his apparent inability to cope with headstrong superstars, something Dennis had managed when he ran Alain Prost and Ayrton Senna, drivers closer to his age at the time, but an attribute that was clearly no longer relevant in 2007. Dennis, previously respected for his integrity, had also dismayed the media by looking economic with the truth when attempting to defend Alonso's actions in the pit lane in Hungary.

Nonetheless, Dennis earned widespread sympathy for the manner in which the so-called spy drama had been blown out of proportion, a notion that did not have the support of Mosley. The president of the FIA claimed that McLaren had got off lightly and the drivers were fortunate not to have been stripped of their championship points. This had been expected because of previous technical irregularities in F1 which had nothing to do with the drivers but for which they had been penalized, along with the team. Mosley explained that he had previously written to all three McLaren drivers (Alonso, Hamilton and de la Rosa), asking for whatever information they either knew or had on their computers. In return, they would be granted amnesty.

But, having let the drivers off, Mosley spiked the conversation with bitterness and controversy by suggesting that if Hamilton won the title, it would be tainted and, in any case, McLaren had polluted both this and future championships, the implication being that McLaren might use Ferrari information on their 2008 car.

In summary, McLaren were not guilty of incorporating Ferrari's details in their car, the MP4/22. The stripping of McLaren's championship points and the imposition of the $100-million fine was for the acquisition of a 'significant sporting advantage', an accusation that scarcely seemed to warrant such a savage penalty.

By the time the news had been received and digested, the majority of F1 personnel had arrived at Spa-Francorchamps. As darkness gathered over the Ardennes, the verdict dominated conversation in the Honda enclave where the British-based team was entertaining the media to pasta and a glass of wine. I had written a blog, which had been posted on the website for *Top Gear*, my first commission for the British magazine. The gist of the piece, based on information available at the time, was that the outrageous punishment most certainly did not fit the crime. These were my words:

Ron Dennis, with his mangled English and slightly superior demeanour, is not the sort of bloke you warm to. But I was not alone in feeling sorry for the McLaren boss as he dealt with the kicking received by the combined forces of Ferrari and the FIA. Given the choice of standing outside the FIA headquarters in Paris to await the World Council decision or travelling to Spa-Francorchamps, I chose the latter. It was a good move because I could gauge the broad reaction in F1 as the verdict came through while the teams prepared for this weekend's Belgian Grand Prix.

It was pretty clear that there would be a penalty of some sort because the FIA had gathered further evidence in the so-called spy scandal. But 'surprise' would be an under-statement when describing the reaction to the news that McLaren had been thrown out of this year's constructors' championship and fined a massive $100 m. The good news was that the drivers' championship remains unaffected. The bad news for McLaren is that they are now regarded as cheats. Why? Well, as I write, I'm not quite sure. A statement from McLaren contained the following key sentence . . .

'We have never denied that the information from Ferrari was in the personal possession of one of our employees at his home. This issue is: was this information used by McLaren? This is not the case and has not been proven today.'

So, if they were not guilty of using the Ferrari informa-tion, what, exactly, is the precise nature of their crime, one that warrants such a draconian penalty?

FIA officials were reported to be pleased with the out-come: 'a neat compromise' was one verdict. This is a reference to the McLaren drivers, Lewis Hamilton and

Fernando Alonso, being unaffected in their fight for the Drivers' Championship. There are two points of view on this one: if McLaren were cheating, then the drivers are part of that team and should be removed from their championship too. On the other hand, the FIA knew that there would have been outrage had the best championship in years been wrecked by such a decision, not to mention removing the chances of Hamilton, the brightest star to have emerged for some time, from winning the title in his debut year. You can see the front pages of the tabloids now; the FIA and its president, Max Mosley, would have been pilloried.

Questions remain. If the FIA are so outraged by McLaren's behaviour, why did they not become involved in the case of two ex-Ferrari employees bringing sensitive information from Maranello to Toyota? Apparently, no complaint was brought by Ferrari, so the FIA were not empowered to investigate. But surely the principle is the same? And what about Colin Kolles, the boss of Spyker, brandishing a drawing leaked from Red Bull as part of Spyker's battle against Toro Rosso using a 'customer car', in this case, last year's Red Bull? Why was nothing said about that?

Oh, and one further point to think about. This entire affair was triggered by a Ferrari employee leaking the information to McLaren. Are Ferrari not responsible for this person in the same way that McLaren have been made culpable for the damaging and stupid actions of Mike Coughlan, their former Chief Designer?

Teams have copied each other's work since Bernie Ecclestone was in short pants but the line has now become blurred between what is acceptable and what is not. McLaren are guilty of something that has not yet been made clear. The feeling here at Spa is that the punishment does not fit the crime and, in the process, F1 has been made to look stupid and out of touch with the real world. Yet again.

After enjoying a glass of red with Honda, I returned to the media centre to begin preparing a piece for the following Sunday's edition of the *Observer*. I left at 11 p.m., in the company of Alan Henry, motor sport correspondent of the *Observer*'s sister paper, the *Guardian*. As we passed the Ferrari motor home, Luca Colajanni suddenly appeared and began to berate me about 'the punishment not fitting the crime'. He caught me unawares because I had only agreed to write for *Top Gear* that morning and had not mentioned my new association with the magazine to anyone. The press officer had clearly been trawling the web for Ferrari mentions and come across the blog. He was as angry as I was surprised. After a heated discussion, the mood gradually calmed. Without saying as much, Colajanni appeared to think my words were the typical overreaction of a British journalist supporting an English-based team. Our spat had summed up the divisive nature of a 'spygate' scandal that was running deep through all sections of the paddock.

With accusations and counter-accusations rife, Dennis called the British media to the Brand Centre for a briefing first thing on Friday morning. Alonso's blackmail attempt in Hungary, hitherto not in the public domain, had become common knowledge. Dennis was attempting to explain it first before answering the question of why he had not sacked the Spaniard on the spot, a point being pursued with enthusiasm and justification by Ed Gorman, the motor sport correspondent of *The Times*.

'Fernando and I had a discussion in Hungary, but I'm not going to give you the details,' said Dennis. 'When he left, I phoned the FIA to tell them what had happened. Half an hour later, his manager told me Fernando was sorry and wanted to retract everything he'd said.

'Then, after the race, Fernando came to me, apologized,

shook my hand and said, "Let's get on with racing." I accepted that.'

Dennis said he had yet to decide whether to appeal against the $100-million fine and the loss of all constructors' championship points. He claimed that the information covering matters such as the Ferrari's weight distribution, brake balance and the team's pit stop tactics in Melbourne was not significant and had no relevance to McLaren. Ferrari argued differently, saying the possession of such sensitive details was a major advantage for a rival, a point with which the WMSC had concurred.

McLaren were unlikely to either appeal to the FIA or take the matter to a civil court. Dennis said that so long as McLaren's shareholders were comfortable with dealing with the fine, he wished to see the matter closed. Dennis claimed he had his best night's sleep in months after the court had reached its verdict. 'I feel that I can now control things again and we can get on with the racing,' said Dennis.

Everything in the FIA document [summarizing the WMSC hearing] is true. True in their content. It happened. But there is only one thing that I feel is not appropriate. This is a fine so disproportionate to the reality of the situation. So the decision I have is not whether to appeal their findings. It is: do I appeal the fine? Does McLaren take a financial hit in the interests of the sport? Once I have reached a decision I will make a recommendation to my shareholders, and it is they who will decide. If we do not appeal this it will be because we want closure.

Do you really think it's a great backdrop for Formula One and my company if we've one-and-a-half to two years of legal aggravation with my management that is not there for that? They are there to focus on making race-winning cars and enter into commercial relationships with sponsors. I have had letters, emails and faxes that have streamed into me over the last twenty-four hours, and every sponsor is committed to staying with this racing team and backing us to the hilt. So I don't want to drag them into it. I don't want to drag this thing out, if I can get closure.

I hope the other teams understand the financial penalty we will swallow in the interests of the sport. The important thing to us is the company's integrity, and the firm belief of the world that we have never competed with a car that has anybody else's technology in it. We want to win fair and square, and if the penalty for that is money – putting aside the [championship] points because it's about money in the end – then that's the penalty. If the perception of the media and the public is that McLaren did not cheat, we did everything we could to cooperate, then we probably will take the financial hit. There is not more than one other team in the pit lane who can take a $100 million hit. At the end of the day, we can swallow it.

Regardless of his wish for closure, the knock-on effect of the affair would continue to remind Dennis of the most embarrassing phase in the forty-one-year history of the McLaren F1 team. While Dennis clearly believed everything he had said to the media about the extent of the infiltration of Ferrari information, the reality would turn out to be very different. In addition, apart from dealing with a disgruntled Alonso for the rest of the season, Dennis would have to think about how to replace him even though Alonso's management insisted in Belgium that the Spaniard would see out the second year of his contract in 2008.

Whoever partnered Hamilton would have to become part of a humbling process that would surely stick in Dennis's craw. F1 hierarchy is determined by the number of constructors' championship points scored each season. The likes of McLaren, Renault and Ferrari usually occupy the smart end of the pit lane, where they are each allocated three garages. In 2008, thanks to having officially scored no points in 2007, McLaren would be at the bottom of the pit lane, attempting to squeeze their vast array of equipment into two small garages alongside Force India and Super Aguri. It would be a comedown similar to the owner of a Victorian detached property moving into a council flat. That would not be a hardship at modern tracks such as Shanghai and Malaysia. But at Interlagos in Brazil, McLaren would find themselves in a narrow cul-de-sac, close by the tyre depot, at the end of the paddock. There would be other restrictions, such as the absence of travel concessions (twenty free air tickets per race and 15 tonnes of subsidized freight for which McLaren would now have to pay $26 per kilogram) and a reduction in the number of paddock and pit lane passes.

Dennis looked tired and drawn. The spygate affair, which had been running for more than two months, had taken its physical toll more severely than the passing of his sixtieth birthday in June. 'No matter how beaten up I am, and no matter how kicked around I am, the fact is that I love F1,' said Dennis. 'Our passion is still for F1. That is our objective . . . and if the right way forward is to act as shareholders in the interests of F1, then we will go down that path.'

Barring serious misfortune in the remaining four races, Ferrari were guaranteed victory in the 2007 constructors' championship. The Italian team stated its satisfaction that the truth had finally emerged at the WMSC hearing. While a number in the paddock at Spa shared Ferrari's view that the McLaren drivers were fortunate to be allowed to remain in the championship, some observers questioned the fact that Ferrari did not receive a reprimand at the very least for being the source of the problem in the first place.

'It's not as if McLaren stole the information,' said Eddie Jordan, the former F1 team owner. 'It was leaked by a Ferrari employee. If McLaren were blamed for Coughlan's actions because he is an employee, then surely Ferrari should be made to take some sort of responsibility for Stepney's actions and the effect they've had on the sport? Ferrari need to take a good look at themselves. It's not the first time information has been leaked from this team.'

Meanwhile, Mosley had arrived at Spa-Francorchamps to give his views on the WMSC verdict. As questioning by the media got into its stride, Mosley seemed slightly nonplussed by the view that the penalty had been harsh and inappropriate. Indeed, he became visibly irritated when asked by David Croft of BBC Radio 5 Live to explain the precise nature of a crime worthy of a $100-million fine.

It said much about the significance of this affair and its handling by the FIA that a return to Spa-Francorchamps after a two-year absence had largely been ignored. Two drivers from Ferrari, along with McLaren's Alonso, sat happily alongside each other at the post-qualifying press conference to provide a welcome counterpoint to the festering hostility between their respective teams. Räikkönen, Massa and Alonso spoke about the more pertinent and realistic business of attempting to win the Belgian Grand Prix.

After being trounced by McLaren at Monza, Ferrari typified this extraordinary seesaw season by returning to top form as Räikkönen and Massa gave the Italian team sole occupancy of the front row for the first time in 2007. Despite the furore surrounding his relationship with McLaren, Alonso was happy to be faster than Hamilton.

The Ferrari drivers needed all the help they could get since Räikkönen and Massa were third and fourth in the championship and fighting for prominence within their own team, never mind the championship. With three races remaining after this fourteenth round of the series, the time would surely come for Ferrari to ask one driver to help the other in the battle with McLaren. Even if a Ferrari driver won at Spa and, say, Hamilton finished third, the Englishman's lead of 18 points over

Räikkönen and 23 over Massa would have been reduced by just 4 points.

The mathematics favoured Räikkönen to receive the nod eventually from the Ferrari management. But that would not prevent Massa from doing everything possible to keep his name in the frame, a situation that pleased McLaren even though the British team faced a similar problem within its own ranks, one that had been exacerbated by revelations concerning the rift between Alonso and Dennis. The Spanish media had been quick to note that their man could be out of favour, an observation that was bringing further pressure to the team.

Alonso's behaviour in Hungary may have startled Dennis but it also sent a message that Hamilton would begin to understand all too clearly during the first lap of the Belgian Grand Prix. Despite his faults, Alonso's desire to win knew no bounds and that, coupled with aggression and outstanding natural ability, looked like being the key as the championship moved into the final three races.

Although Ferrari dominated in Belgium, Hamilton came away with the equally uncomfortable thought that, for the second race in succession, he had no answer to Alonso's speed as they finished third and fourth. It was here that Alonso's experience, gained during 102 Grands Prix, was coming into play as he worked on the fine detail of the mechanical and aerodynamic set-up of his car. More significantly, perhaps, he had made his policy of non-communication with Dennis work in his favour as he desisted from the public moaning that had affected his early season efforts.

As they had fought for third place just after the start, Alonso had used the entire road to force Hamilton on to the asphalt run-off area on the outside of the corner. It had been a marginal move but one which was typical of the forceful driving to be expected on the first lap, and at such a critical stage in the season. It prompted a hair-raising moment as the silver cars then ran side-by-side, downhill at 180 m.p.h. towards the switchback sequence at Eau Rouge. Neither driver had wanted to back off but, in the end, Hamilton had no option in the face of Alonso's unflinching determination.

Hamilton had lost out, which was no disgrace under the circumstances. His only mistake was to protest in public and let Alonso know he was rattled. Suddenly, the emphasis had changed. Hitherto the Spaniard had shown plentiful signs of being flustered by the unexpected pace of his inexperienced team-mate, a bonus for Hamilton as he had continued to dominate the championship. Now the boot was on the other foot. The gap had been reduced to just 2 points as the teams headed from Belgium to Japan. Hamilton, meanwhile, had a plan.

When the race engineers arrived for work at McLaren on the Monday after Spa, they were surprised to find Hamilton waiting in the office. Determined to learn even more about getting the most from the MP4/22, Hamilton set to work on a detailed analysis of his performances in Italy and Belgium. He had followed a different path to Alonso when setting up his car and, clearly, this had not worked. Two days later, Hamilton emerged from the McLaren Technical Centre feeling he knew where he had gone wrong. Even if Hamilton played golf, his hectic schedule would not have permitted time for a game. In 1986, Nigel Mansell's clubs had never been far from reach.

23
Mexican Two-Step

Nigel Mansell finished his first day of practice for the Portuguese Grand Prix, took time for a quick word with his team and then headed for the golf course. This was in the days before an army of technicians, umbilically linked to banks of computers in support vehicles at the back of a F1 garage, would produce reams of statistics for the driver to pore over endlessly with his engineer. It was late September and the fairways at Estoril Sol proved more tempting than hanging around a dusty, tumbledown paddock.

A game of golf seemed the natural follow-on in a schedule that read like a page from *Boys' Own* magazine. In the fortnight since finishing second at Monza, Mansell had flown with the Red Arrows and, a few days later, sat alongside Tony Pond as the rally driver hustled his Metro 6R4 through the narrow lanes used for the Manx Rally. Such a thing would be most unlikely today, if not because of the risk of injury in a rally car, then because of the clashing interest of whichever motor manufacturer supported the F1 driver's team. Climbing into an Austin Rover would not be the done thing for a driver associated with the likes of Mercedes-Benz or Renault. As far as Mansell was concerned, the joy rides and the golf were a perfect opportunity to relax as the championship reached the final three races with four drivers vying for the title.

Mansell led Piquet by 5 points. It was a deceptive margin

since the points structure in 1986 allowed each driver to count only his best eleven results from sixteen. Mansell had accumulated his 61 points by scoring in ten races; Piquet had claimed 56 in just eight Grands Prix. Prost was even worse off than Mansell, having consistently picked up 53 points in ten races. Senna, a further 5 points in arrears, at least had the consolation provided by the unreliable Lotus giving him just eight scoring finishes. As far as Mansell was concerned, the simplest solution would be to win the race and then reassess the situation. Which is exactly what he did.

In one of his most important and impressive victories thus far, Mansell led from start to finish. Prost took second, with Piquet third, the hard-luck story belonging to Senna. Holding second place at the start of the final lap, his Lotus ran out of fuel. At Senna's final pit stop, the on-board fuel read-out had shown that consumption was marginally too high. Senna drove with that in mind and tripped the figure on to the correct side. When the Renault engine coughed its last, the cockpit reading said he had 1.4 laps of fuel remaining. That error not only cost Senna a place on the podium, it also eliminated him from the title chase. Mansell, meanwhile, knew that a repeat performance at the penultimate round in Mexico would deliver the championship. Indeed, if he finished anywhere ahead of his two remaining rivals, the job would be done. If only life were that simple.

It would be a long haul to Mexico City, the F1 teams venturing into the unknown as this race returned to the calendar after a lengthy absence. Encouraged by their government in the early Sixties, the Comité Directivo Gran Premio de México gained permission to build a permanent racetrack within Magdalena Mixhuca, a municipal park in the suburbs of the sprawling city. The committee's enthusiasm was encouraged by the presence of Ricardo Rodríguez in F1, the 20-year-old Mexican having signed for Ferrari in 1962. When a non-championship race in Mexico was planned for November of that year, Ferrari chose not to enter thanks to the uncompetitive state of their cars. Rodríguez found a drive with a privately entered Lotus, a move that would have a tragic end. Rodríguez lost control during practice, hit the guardrail at the top of the final corner, a banked curve, and was thrown from the car. Rodríguez died of his injuries in front of his parents, brother Pedro and an adoring public.

Despite such a terrible start to Mexico's first official connection with F1, the race was granted championship status the following year and remained part of the series until a chaotic race in 1970. The track had been named Autódromo Ricardo Rodríguez in honour of the nation's young hero but the enthusiasm of 200,000 locals went unchecked as they climbed the grass banks and sat on the edge of the track. Despite pleas from Jackie Stewart and Pedro Rodríguez (now an F1 driver with BRM), the spectators remained resolute. Fearing a riot if the race was cancelled, the drivers reluctantly took the start on a track that was effectively lined by human barriers. Stewart retired when his Tyrrell hit a dog and, after 65 laps, the chequered flag brought the race to a halt – for ever, it seemed.

That did not take into account the tireless enthusiasm of the Mexicans for motor racing. Ten million dollars was spent on a massive revamp of the circuit, renamed Autódromo Hermanos Rodríguez (to include Pedro, who had been killed in a sports car race in 1971). Layers of fencing, some with barbed wire, were installed to keep the crowd at bay although a price tag of $115 for a three-day ticket acted as a strong deterrent on its own. A crowd of 50,000, enthusiastic but orderly, turned up on 12 October to witness the return of F1 to their country and the probable crowning of Nigel Mansell as 1986 world champion.

The British press travelled to Mexico, a considerable number for the day although nothing like the twenty or so journalists regularly attending the races in 2007. In the absence of official FIA press conferences, a meeting with Mansell was arranged, for reasons that still remain unclear, in the airport. To complicate matters further, the area chosen was airside, thus involving the journalists with security passes and checks before getting close to the great man – in a café.

Mansell had been complaining of stomach trouble, the result, he believed, of a BBC dinner celebrating Murray Walker's sixty-third birthday. Sickness was a regular affliction for visitors to Mexico City and one that Piquet craftily capitalized on by choosing his moment to remove the toilet roll from the only lavatory in the Williams garage.

On a more serious and technical level, the Lotus team had been stung by reports suggesting that their car, which had given Senna eight pole positions thus far in 1986, was somehow illegal in qualifying trim. A statement from John Player Special Team Lotus refuted the notion and pointed out that the car was checked regularly by the FIA scrutineers. The statement concluded:

> The team feels that these continuing stories seriously detract from the outstanding merit of these performances: – (1) by the driver, Ayrton Senna, recognized as one of the fastest and most outstanding drivers, who in 31 Grands Prix with the team has achieved 15 pole positions, (2) by the technicians and mechanics of the team who have a great pride in their work, (3) by the superb engine supplied by Renault Sport, which yesterday achieved the 50th pole position for that company.
>
> The defamatory and derogatory statements must now either:
> (1) Stop
> OR
> (2) Be supported by an official protest as provided for in the Sporting Regulations
> OR

(3) Be answered by the persons making them when Team
Lotus will be forced to seek recompense for the
damage to its reputation.

Within a matter of hours, Williams issued a statement:

> Canon Williams Honda wishes to state that at no time has it
> accused any team competing in the 1986 FISA World
> Championship of entering an illegal car. If it did believe a
> car was illegal, a protest would be lodged.
>
> In winning nine Grands Prix and securing the 1986
> Constructors' Championship, Canon Williams Honda has
> the utmost confidence in the FISA-appointed scrutineers
> and their ability to pinpoint irregularities amongst compet-
> ing cars.

This technical swordplay was hardly discussed by the British
media. Something far more juicy and newsworthy had arrived
the previous day from London. The only fax in the media centre
had clicked into life on 11 October. Stuttering laboriously
through the machine came a copy of a feature written by James
Hunt and published in *The Times* that morning. Commenting on
the fact that Mansell could become the first British champion
since Hunt had won the title ten years before, the 1976 world
champion claimed that success for Mansell would not be well
received by those inside F1. The feeling, according to Hunt, was
that Mansell was not fit to be a worthy champion.

There was immediate outrage, particularly among the journalists who had been flown to Mexico to sing Mansell's praises.
Here was a retired champion tearing apart the reputation of a
driver on the point of achieved lasting greatness. How dare he?
As the initial shock subsided and the article became the subject
of discussion over coffee in the paddock, there began a creeping
realization that others quietly shared Hunt's views and he had

merely been bold enough to articulate them in print. To some, however, this was a betrayal; the exposure of a skeleton in the F1 cupboard. Mansell, with his persecution complex and a willingness to complain, was not always popular. The story was divisive: either you supported Mansell or you did not. There were no half measures, which was appropriate because that was the way the Englishman drove his car. For all his faults, Mansell was a racer par excellence. And this had the potential to be the greatest weekend of a spectacular career.

Hunt was present in Mexico in his role as summarizer for BBC Television, a rare turn of events for BBC commentators who usually covered faraway races from the studio in London. Indeed, it was considered something of a step forward that, according to *Autosport*, the BBC would give 'extensive coverage' by showing ten minutes of the early part of the race and then a full thirty minutes live at the finish. BBC Radio 2 would provide a race report from Simon Taylor in Mexico between 22.45 and 23.00 on Sunday evening. And that would be it. In the event, there would be quite a bit to say. Particularly during the opening 10 seconds.

With Senna on pole and Piquet starting alongside his fellow Brazilian, Mansell lined up third, directly behind the Lotus. Berger had qualified fourth in the Benetton while Prost, very much the outsider and hardly mentioned in the pro-Mansell hype, would start his McLaren from sixth. If Mansell, with a 10-point advantage in his pocket, could get ahead of Piquet and stay there, then the title would be his and he would care little about what Hunt or anyone else had to say.

The conditions were hot and sultry as the twenty-five cars rolled on to the grid. The red light came on and then, as was the case in 1986, the green. Twenty-four cars surged forward. Mansell remained stationary. Unable to find first gear, Mansell selected second and by the time he had struggled off the line, most of the field had miraculously avoided the Williams, leaving Mansell languishing in eighteenth place. His qualifying effort had been squandered. Now began a typical Mansell charge as he passed eight cars in 10 laps. At the front, Piquet led Senna with Prost moving into third, ahead of Berger.

Mansell paid the price for his strong pace in the early laps when a blistered front tyre necessitated an early pit stop before rejoining in thirteenth place. Tyres, in fact, would be the deciding factor. While the drivers using Goodyear – the majority of the field in fact – would need to stop at least once, the Pirelli tyres on the Benetton could last for the entire 68 laps. Berger bided his time and gradually moved forward to take his first F1 victory. Significantly, in terms of the championship, Prost managed to get by on two sets of tyres whereas Piquet stopped three times and Mansell twice. Prost, having used his guile and sensitive touch to advantage, claimed a very important second place to move to within 6 points of Mansell. Piquet kept his name in the frame by finishing fourth but an eventual fifth place was of no use to Mansell since he would have to drop the 2 points.

When the race was over, Mansell left for the airport without speaking to the media, a press release offering no reason for the fumbled start that had cost him so dearly. There would be no time for a restorative game of golf but Mansell could use the flight home to ponder that he remained the favourite for the final round in Australia. He could also use the time to consider the self-inflicted complications that he had brought to his life.

A decision to remain with Williams for another two years had provoked outrage at Ferrari, where it was claimed Mansell had met Enzo Ferrari and signed a contract halfway through the season. A statement from Maranello laid bare the facts. According to Mr Ferrari:

We did not solicit the services of Mansell. We were approached by him. I met Mansell here at Maranello on July 17 [the week following the British Grand Prix] and he signed a regular agreement, which we have, and which defines everything, even the number of tickets required by him for each Grand Prix.

His subsequent behaviour has amazed us and our lawyer will treat the matter in the appropriate manner. This does not alter our great admiration of Mansell as a driver but it does show us the kind of person with whom we would have been dealing.

We had our discussions with Mansell because he assured us that he had no future plans with our friend Frank Williams, to whom we renew our good wishes.

Williams sprang to Mansell's defence, pointing out that he had merely signed the minutes of the meeting at Maranello. A contract, which had arrived at Mansell's office not long after, remained unsigned.

In the unlikely event of Lewis Hamilton having been involved in something similar in 2007, the respective lawyers would have taken matters more seriously and less overtly. But, whatever the legal procedure, Ferrari would have been highly unlikely to send McLaren their good wishes. Such a benevolent gesture was not the way of the Maranello regime in 2007.

24

Japanese
Takeaway

Lewis Hamilton was not going to lose sleep over anything that did not affect driving the McLaren. In fact, he was going to bed earlier than usual and rising an hour before normal, the better to get his body in tune with the time difference between Britain and Japan. One of the few disappointments associated with this trip would be the final destination at the Mount Fuji track rather than Suzuka. Hamilton had heard a great deal about Suzuka, the only figure-of-eight circuit in F1. Suzuka may have been long in the tooth but, perhaps for that reason, it was considered to be a serious challenge because the circuit possessed every conceivable type of corner, some of which would not be considered suitable for the more clinical facilities introduced in the twenty-first century. Now they had taken Suzuka away.

Suzuka had one small problem; it was owned by Honda. That might not have caused any difficulties for the majority of teams but Toyota found it uncomfortable listening to the eulogies heaped on a treasure owned by their great rival. The simplest solution for Toyota would be to purchase their own track. In 2000, the motor giant added the circuit at Mount Fuji to its assets, initiated a major revamp and placed a successful application to stage the Grand Prix in 2007.

Mount Fuji, a couple of hours' drive from Tokyo, already had a brief but controversial F1 history. The first of two Japanese

235

Chequered Conflict

Grands Prix had settled the 1976 world championship, a significant occasion that was almost washed out by atrocious weather. Hunt and Lauda had continued their fight, a contest that had become more extraordinary by the race as Hunt had his British Grand Prix victory removed on a technicality in a courtroom, only for the Englishman to recoup much of the 17-point deficit with two exceptional back-to-back wins at Mosport in Canada and Watkins Glen in the USA. When they reached Japan for the final race, Lauda led Hunt by just 3 points.

On race day, it rained, as only it can in this part of Japan. There were doubts that the race would run. Unlike 2007, there were no contingency plans to allow the field to start the race at a modest pace behind the Safety Car. It would be all or nothing. After much dithering, the race was on even though the conditions, if anything, had deteriorated. Hunt made the most of pole position and shot into the lead. Lauda, meanwhile, was going backwards through the field. Having been at death's door, Lauda's values were different from those of the drivers around him. After a few laps, Lauda decided against continuing and pulled into the pits, seemingly handing the title to his rival.

All Hunt needed to do was finish in the top four. That became a problem when he suffered a puncture and dived into the pits thinking that all had been lost. Hunt returned to the track and drove as if there would be no tomorrow, so much so that he passed two cars without realizing he had moved into third place. When the race came to an end, Hunt, convinced he had lost, erupted from the cockpit, only to be confronted by a sea of smiling faces. He was world champion.

The following year, Fuji made its mark for different reasons when a car barrel-rolled off the track and crashed into a group of marshals and photographers, killing two of them. That was the last time F1 had visited this venue. The return in 2007 was not anticipated with great enthusiasm. But that did not allow for Toyota's handsome investment.

Not only had the pits and paddock been rebuilt from scratch, the track layout had also been modified at one point to provide an interesting and tricky sequence of corners leading on to one of the longest straights in F1. Under normal circumstances, the drivers' first impressions after investigating the track on foot and by scooter would have been top of the media agenda. But these were not normal circumstances.

The 'spygate' scandal continued to act like a festering sore on the back of a wonderful championship. A driver's opinion about the severity of turn 8 could not compete with the explosive package of words neatly bundled up in a press release and delivered, one suspected, with a certain amount of feigned innocence by the FIA. In the continuing interest of openness and transparency, the governing body had made public the transcript of the World Motor Sport Council hearing on 13 September. For Ron Dennis, the nightmare was continuing as his comments on Fernando Alonso entered every salacious discussion worthy of the name. After this, there could be no more pretence that all was sweetness and light within McLaren. Dennis told the hearing when referring to Alonso in the aftermath of the Hungarian race:

We are not on speaking terms, but that does not matter. We have not had any conversations since that point.

First, the relationship between Fernando and myself is extremely cold. That is an understatement. In Fernando's mind, there is the firm belief that our policy, whereby each driver receives equal treatment, does not properly reflect his status as world champion. He bases this assertion on the fact that his experience and knowledge and what came to him from his former team is such that he should receive an advantage.

In that discussion [on race morning in Hungary], he was extremely upset with what had taken place the previous day, but nowhere nearly as upset as I was. He said things that he subsequently and fully retracted. Within the passage of material, he made a specific reference to emails from a McLaren engineer. When he made this statement, I said, 'Stop.' I went out, brought Mr Whitmarsh in, and Fernando said everything again, in front of his manager.

When he had finished, I turned to Martin Whitmarsh, asking what we should do with this particular part of the conversation. Martin said we should find Max. After Martin and Fernando left, that is exactly what we did. I recounted the entire conversation to Max. I was upset and angry, but mainly upset. Max calmed me down.

He said that I should do nothing. I started to calm down. Then, prior to the race, Fernando's manager came and said that Fernando had lost his temper and completely retracted everything he said. When I phoned Max, Max was understanding and said things to me that are irrelevant here, though I would be more than comfortable sharing them.

He was completely understanding and said that, on the basis of what I told him, if he felt there was any real validity in what Fernando had said, he would contact me prior to taking any action. However, on the basis that this was an engineering matter, I asked Martin whether he thought something was amiss in that area. He told me, 'We have been too thorough in talking to the engineers; he cannot have been telling the truth.' We subsequently had a reasonable Grand Prix.

Fernando came to me. He had come in third. He apologized for the outburst and I put it down to the heat of the moment, in which he was angry. That is how I took it. Other than following up with Martin, the matter ended there, until twenty-six days later, when the drivers received a letter [from the FIA, offering amnesty in return for information]. What took place between those times, I do not know. I do not know what circumstances brought that into the public domain.

Dennis also revealed that McLaren had asked Alonso to attend the Paris hearing, but the Spaniard had refused to go.

'Mr Alonso is not here because he does not want to be here,' said Dennis. 'He does not speak to anyone much. He is a remarkable recluse for a driver. He is not here by choice. Moreover, he said he had other things to do by previous arrangement. I cannot force him to come. We asked him to come.'

After a measured start to his response, it became clear Alonso was not going to take this slight on his character without passing comment. Not long after arriving at Mount Fuji he said:

About the spying I have nothing to say . . . I will try to speak on the track and try to do my job. I really think that many of the things that have been said about the spying and about me are totally wrong and not the truth. But these things happen and I will not answer every day what they have been saying about me and about anything, I will not lose time on that.

I cannot be every day and every week answering rumours and telling my point of view or my version or my truth to anyone. I will not tell every day what's true and what's not true. But in this case, for example, it's not true. I was surprised about that comment because in Spa we were talking together in the hotel [after the hearing] and I read in the press that we were not talking and I don't know. If Ron said that, it's because he wanted [to].

Press briefings at McLaren on a Thursday had become a standard part of the race weekend, the drivers having between five and ten minutes with their respective national media representatives. Since this was the fifteenth round of the championship and only the hard core of serious F1 media had travelled to Japan, Hamilton had become familiar and relaxed with those present. Perhaps, on this occasion, too relaxed. Hamilton had been so focused on restoring the status quo after defeat by Alonso in Belgium and Italy – and being unaware of the fall-out from the WMSC transcript – he did not realize the loaded nature of the question when asked if, in his opinion, Alonso been loyal enough to McLaren.

'No,' said Hamilton matter-of-factly. 'I think the team have gone out of their way . . . as Fernando has been the world champion coming into the team, especially at the beginning of the season he's the guy that's supposed to take them to the championship, and they've bent over backwards to make him feel comfortable. Me and Pedro have done the same, we've been told: "Try and make Fernando feel welcome in the team." We've done that, and then you saw what he did to the team,' said Hamilton, referring to Alonso not attending the Paris hearing. That was Hamilton's thought on the matter. It was also the makings of another strong story for the following day's newspapers as the championship rivalry was ramped up even further.

Reading these words on the websites and listening to the gossip while pursuing a new life racing in the United States, Juan Pablo Montoya was qualified to pass judgement on the apparent willingness of the world he had left behind to self-destruct. Having spent almost five years in F1 with Williams and McLaren before moving to NASCAR racing, Montoya was scarcely surprised. He told Associated Press:

> It's just how Formula One is. Teams are allowed to bend the rules too much. That's just my personal opinion, but I always felt like people bent the rules and that some teams were allowed to bend the rules more than others. But this? This is crossing the line. Someone is always cheating. All the teams have photographers who take pictures of everything on the car. Everybody does it.

Here in NASCAR, you have the car right next door to you, you can see it and everything on it. But in F1, if someone tried a new wing or something, everyone would go and take pictures of it. A million pictures of the wing at every angle and then they'd put it on the wind tunnel and go try it. Everyone copies. It's just the way F1 works. There are so many ways for people to bend the rules.

Unlike the FIA, Montoya believed the emails between Alonso and de la Rosa were neither unusual nor significant.

'The crazy thing about the emails is they aren't really that big a deal because you can always find out what everybody else is running,' said Montoya. 'Somebody will always open their mouth. You go for dinner, and somebody will say "We're running this weight and doing that." So, most of the time, you can find out what people are running anyway. And de la Rosa was always like that. He would call people and tell them.'

In the meantime, McLaren decided not to appeal against the $100-million fine and the stripping of championship points.

'We believe the time has come to put this huge distraction behind us,' said Dennis. 'It's in the best interests of the sport. McLaren wants to win races and world championships. We are fortunate to have, and continue to receive, unwavering support from our employees, sponsor partners and F1 fans across the world – all of whom are equally keen that we totally focus on winning this year's drivers' championship and the remaining three races of the season.'

That seemed a reasonable ambition. Hamilton led Alonso by 2 points with Räikkönen a further 11 points in arrears. Massa, 20 points behind Hamilton, would need serious misfortune to strike the other three. But, given the way the season had been going, coupled with a forecast for poor weather at Fuji, nothing could be ruled out.

25

Hamilton Wins,
Alonso Spins

When Lewis Hamilton discussed the championship, although he did not say as much, it was clear that he saw Alonso as his only rival. Mount Fuji in Japan may have been unfamiliar to all of the contenders but Hamilton recognized Alonso's advantage going into the final two races in China and Brazil.

He knows Shanghai very well, and he knows Interlagos very well, but that has never stopped me from beating him in other places so I am not worried. It's difficult to say what is going to happen at this race or the next race. Either of us could have a bad race and that could really spice things up. The key for me is just to make sure that I finish in the top three, get as many points as possible, and preferably win.

I've been working hard since the last race trying to understand where I can find time and where I have been losing time, and I understand it now. So, I have a feeling that this weekend will be a lot better than the previous few. I am feeling relaxed and we have made some good steps forward in the car as well.

Usually Fernando and I have similar set-ups, and more often than not it is the set-up I found from tests. I do the first day and a half, find a set-up and then Pedro or Fernando turn up and drive my car. Then they either like it or make some changes to it.

So then we go to a race and we have got a very similar set-up or they have tweaked it a little bit. At the last race especially [in Belgium] I went somewhere else on my set-up, thinking it was the right way and we were wrong. It was miles apart and, although I was not that far off his times, I feel that if my set-up was a lot further in the other direction it would have been a lot better.

When you go through the Friday practice, you haven't got much time to change it, or take big risks, so you go into qualifying and you are stuck with what you have got. You can't always get it right, and I definitely didn't get it right in the last races.

After a week of oral shadow boxing with his team-mate – Hamilton having responded to Alonso's continuing claims for preference within the team by saying he did not ask for, and neither did he need, special treatment – Hamilton winded Alonso with a sharp body punch when he qualified on pole position. With the McLaren drivers having claimed the front row, Hamilton's lap may not have been the uppercut that finished off Alonso's championship chances but it was a beautifully timed and executed blow. When Räikkönen qualified third, the title fight appeared to continue edging towards being the exclusive preserve of the McLaren drivers.

Adding increased significance to Hamilton's fifth pole, qualifying had been run in foul conditions. The drizzle and fog had been so severe that the free practice session on Saturday had been restricted to all but a few minutes' running thanks to the medical helicopter being unable to operate in such poor visibility. This provided an unwelcome headache for the teams since they had to tackle qualifying later in the day with no information on the performance of rain tyres and the set-up of the car for the wet conditions, Friday's practice having been run in the dry.

The perfect conditions on the first day had at least allowed a rare glimpse of Mount Fuji, the dormant volcano that overlooks the track. Hamilton may have set the fastest time in the dry on Friday but he knew that would count for nothing when qualifying began in the wet. Having been beaten by Alonso in the previous two races and then, inadvertently or otherwise, joined the game of psychological warfare by questioning Alonso's loyalty to the McLaren, Hamilton knew his actions on the track had to speak even louder than some of his ill-advised words. His brilliant final lap was to have a greater effect than any attempt at withering criticism that somehow did not ring true from a 22-year-old who appeared to be speaking out of bravado rather than angry conviction. Hamilton was happy to admit that his daring efforts in the slippery conditions were a match for the efforts of his team:

A very good qualifying for me – and also for the team. I really like the Fuji circuit. We looked strong already during practice when it was dry. Obviously, today's wet conditions made it a very challenging session, particularly as this morning's free practice had been cancelled, all of which makes today's result even more satisfying. The car ran perfectly, and the team has done a great job in making sure we were as prepared as possible. Even though we have not been here before, there was no guesswork involved; nothing in F1 is guesswork. There is a big group of engineers back in England analysing the data. Their calculations were so good that we were immediately very close to the ideal set-up for the car in both the wet and the dry. I really have to thank them for that.

The McLaren-Mercedes team would not thank either of their drivers if Hamilton and Alonso clashed at the first corner, a very tight right-hander similar to La Source at Spa-Francorchamps, where Alonso had forced Hamilton across a kerb. Hamilton had since said that he was prepared to fight fire with fire, now that he knew the true character of his team-mate.

As the rain continued into Sunday morning, the question was whether there would be a race at all. Choosing the option to have the Grand Prix started behind the Safety Car, Race Director Charlie Whiting ran the cars in this manner for 19 laps, each lap counting towards the planned total of 67. When Whiting finally released the field, trouble began at the first corner – but not, as predicted, between the McLaren drivers. Jenson Button and Nick Heidfeld collided as they disputed sixth place, triggering other drivers to run wide. Hamilton held his lead despite an attack from Alonso as they dealt with cold tyres and brakes. Ferrari, meanwhile, appeared to be writing themselves out of the championship.

A late decision by the FIA to have every driver use the so-called extreme wet tyre in such conditions had been passed by email to the teams. Ferrari would later claim not to have received the email until after the race had started, which explained why Räikkönen and Massa, third and fourth fastest in qualifying, had been fitted with the normal wet tyre. When ordered by the FIA to stop and change to extreme wets, the Ferrari drivers fell to the back of the field. It would be the prelude to an impressive climb back to an eventual third as Räikkönen clung to the championship by his fingertips. Massa would be written out of the title fight after finishing sixth.

All of this added extra emphasis to the battle between the McLaren drivers at the front. The crucial moment came at the first pit stop. Alonso, lying 3 seconds behind, pitted first, Hamilton coming in on the next lap. The difference was that Alonso rejoined behind a four-car battle for fourth whereas Hamilton got out just ahead of this group. From that moment on, Alonso appeared to lose the rhythm necessary for consistently quick times in such appalling conditions. Nine laps later, he crashed spectacularly.

Hamilton Wins, Alonso Spins

It was true that the Toro Rosso of Sebastian Vettel had damaged the right-rear corner of Alonso's car after an over-enthusiastic attack. But Hamilton had been through similar difficulties when, after his pit stop, he failed to see Kubica coming alongside in the streaming conditions. Hamilton was lucky to be able to continue after a half-spin in company with the BMW, the Englishman dropping pace for several laps as he tried to determine the extent of possible damage caused by a vibration from the rear of his car. When the team reported that nothing was showing on the telemetry, Hamilton pressed on. Alonso had not been so lucky, his wrecked car, beached on the track, bringing out the Safety Car once more.

It was during this interlude that another incident took place as Vettel, making a novice misjudgement, ran into the back of Mark Webber's second-place Red Bull. Vettel, who looked set for a surprise podium in the Toro Rosso, was beside himself with remorse as he limped into the pits to retire.

When the Safety Car was withdrawn, Hamilton now had to fend off an attack by Heikki Kovalainen, but the McLaren pulled away, leaving Kovalainen to worry about the fast-approaching Räikkönen, who had made excellent progress from the back of the field. The Ferrari and the Renault swapped places on the last lap, Kovalainen retaking second place immediately after his fellow-countryman had briefly moved ahead.

This was Hamilton's fourth win and, without question, his best so far. The drive in such appalling conditions had been reminiscent of Senna's first F1 victory in the wet in Portugal in 1985 when the Brazilian had been in a class of his own. Hamilton had shown similar qualities by never putting a foot wrong, even when under pressure. With two races to go, he led Alonso by 12 points and Räikkönen by 17, a seemingly impossible margin for the Ferrari driver to recover. Given the relentless sequence of sometimes incongruous events in 2007, we should have known better than to assume the obvious.

26
Bang Out of Order

Lewis Hamilton arrived in Shanghai believing that a difficult but immaculate drive in Japan was safely behind him. Better than that, he could win the world championship if he either won in China or finished either side of Alonso. It seemed a perfectly reasonable goal. By the Thursday, however, Hamilton's Japanese victory was being put in doubt because of questions about his behaviour when following the Safety Car as marshals dealt with Alonso's crashed McLaren. It was suggested that Hamilton's driving had been erratic and he was to be investigated. This was four days after the race at Fuji was supposedly done and dusted.

Alonso immediately grabbed this opportunity to make veiled remarks about Hamilton's driving as they had prepared to take the start in Japan after 19 laps behind the Safety Car. Hamilton had been concerned about Alonso seizing the moment to snatch the lead when the field was released for the first time. There was the additional problem of keeping his brakes warm and clearing the engine of water, Hamilton, along with all of the drivers, alternately accelerating and braking. At one point, while trying not to be left trailing, Alonso had been caught out as Hamilton suddenly braked, the Spaniard having no alternative but to overtake in order to avoid piling into the back of his team-mate. Then, no sooner had Alonso braked, than Hamilton accelerated again. Hamilton's actions were dramatic, to say the least. It was as if he was recalling Alonso's tactics at the first corner at Spa and was taking no prisoners. Alonso had no hesitation in mentioning all of this in China a few days later.

The subject had been raised by Toro Rosso as the Italian team sought to remove Vettel's ten-place grid penalty for his part in the collision with Webber. New evidence had come light – and this is where an occasionally bizarre season had become even wackier – thanks to a Japanese spectator's film posted on YouTube. Taken from a grandstand, the murky pictures showed Hamilton pulling off the racing line and almost coming to a halt on the extreme right of the track in order to avoid the Safety Car and get a run to clear the Mercedes engine and warm the brakes. This had been enough to distract Vettel, who thought Hamilton had a problem. By the time Vettel, on the left-hand side of the track, had looked to the front again, he was confronted by Webber's slowing Red Bull. A collision was inevitable.

Hamilton had previously been asking his team to have Webber drop back and not run so close to the McLaren. It was an unfortunate sequence of events but Hamilton's cause was not helped by Webber declaring that the McLaren driver had done 'a shit job' when leading the field and keeping a constant pace behind the Safety Car. All of this added to the build up in tension before a car had so much as turned a wheel in China.

In an appalling piece of management, the FIA strung out the story for twenty-four hours, the dripping of information and suggested penalties adding unnecessary stress and hype all round. Predictably, the British media went berserk, the *Sun* going straight to the heart of the matter, as ever, by suggesting that the FIA was not fit to run a garage in Chipping Sodbury.

Toro Rosso achieved their aim by having Vettel's penalty rescinded. After a meeting involving the stewards hearing Hamilton's evidence and peering at the YouTube footage, the Briton's name was cleared. This had taken place behind smoked-glass windows on the ground floor of the control tower. Unfortunately for the officials, the early and fast fall of evening had removed every aspect of privacy previously afforded by the darkened windows, the interior lighting providing full exposure of the stewards at work while in complete ignorance of the curious but delighted media watching from outside.

The stewards had reached exactly the same conclusion as the officials in Japan when reviewing the difficulties imposed by the atrocious conditions. Hamilton's innocence was no more of a surprise than the apparent stage-managing of a championship that had already generated enough drama to fill a book. The difference this time was that those in charge had pushed F1's credibility too far. It took a brilliant lap from Hamilton during qualifying to return the sport to its more realistic values as he claimed pole position, his sixth and arguably the most significant of the season.

Hamilton admitted that the waiting had perhaps affected his preparations on track during Friday's practice, when he was the slowest of the three drivers remaining in the title chase. Eventually freed of any fear of either losing 10 points for his win in Japan or being penalized ten grid places, Hamilton's relief was clear as he left his best lap until the very end of qualifying to beat Räikkönen by a tenth of a second, the Ferrari driver continuing to retain a slim chance of the championship.

Alonso, meanwhile, was giving full vent to a frustration that had gnawed at the world champion ever since the first race of the season. Alonso said his car felt fine during qualifying and he was sure that his best lap had been good enough to win pole, or at least be close to it. 'I was really surprised when they told me that I was fourth fastest. I don't know why this has happened,' said Alonso.

He had used stronger language as he climbed from his car and threw his crash helmet across the garage before punching an office door off its hinges. Alonso claimed that he was not half a second slower than any of his rivals, the inference being that the fault lay with his car and, apparently, its tyre pressures. In the unofficial view of Hamilton's supporters, Alonso seemed to ignore the patently obvious fact that his team-mate had warmed his tyres properly and had been blindingly quick.

Words had become just as important as activity on the track. In a season that seemed to be driven from one crisis to another by an endless sequence of soundbites and statements, Max Mosley was continuing to make contributions that seemed more malevolent than magisterial. Having offered the opinion that the championship would be tainted by the spy scandal if Hamilton won it, Mosley became deeply offensive when answering trenchant criticism of the FIA by Sir Jackie Stewart. In an interview with Jon McEvoy of the *Daily Mail*, Mosley referred to the triple world champion and winner of twenty-seven Grands Prix as 'a certified half-wit' who dressed 'like a 1930s music hall man', a reference to Stewart's penchant for tartan trousers and wearing hats bearing allegiance to RBS, with whom the Scotsman had an ambassadorial role.

Mosley's extraordinary on-the-record outburst was the talk of the paddock. Kevin Garside, motor sport correspondent for the *Daily Telegraph*, summed up the FIA president.

'Formula One is simply too small for Mosley's rampant intellect and vibrant imagination,' wrote Garside. 'He has widened the scope of his role by adding a political dimension through the FIA's global work in road safety. But episodically, on quiet days, he drifts into mischief. Stewart and Hamilton were unfortunate targets.'

Not long after, Damon Hill, the 1996 world champion, wrote a letter to *Autosport*, expressing 'indignation and outrage at the abuse' directed by Mosley at Stewart. This was an unexpected but welcome attack from a mild-mannered man as Hill summed up the feelings of disgust in Shanghai and further afield.

After months of this bitterness, a discussion on Hamilton's attributes would provide a welcome and positive diversion at a press conference featuring a few of the team bosses.

'I could never have imagined a rookie driver to be fighting at the level of competitiveness Hamilton has been doing, he is very special,' said Sir Frank Williams, whose team had won seven drivers' titles. 'Once every ten years or so they come along like Ayrton [Senna] and Michael [Schumacher]. It is very rare and a fantastic event. A story for Formula One.'

Bernie Ecclestone, questioned in the paddock, was in no doubt about Hamilton's role in raising the profile of F1 after years of Schumacher's domination.

He has been a real breath of fresh air and has resurrected F1. I have been in motor racing longer than I care to remember but I've never seen anyone like him. He has been nothing short of a miracle worker. We lost a big hero in Michael Schumacher but in Lewis, we have another. But for him, I'm not sure where the sport would be leading.

It's painfully obvious to me that the right guy to be world champion is Lewis. In fact, my main fear would be if Hamilton didn't win it. Kimi Räikkönen barely talks to anyone and as such has done little for the sport, and as for Fernando Alonso, in his two years as world champion he has done nothing. He hasn't really been an F1 campaigner at all, but if Lewis wins the drivers' championship, he will act like a real world champion. He will know exactly what is expected of him and what he has to do.

Even Jean Todt, in the midst of continually pouring scorn on McLaren and that team's accomplishments, found time to recognize Hamilton's achievement. 'Normally a very talented driver in their first year in F1 doesn't drive for a winning team with a winning car,' said the Ferrari CEO. 'That was the opportunity he had and he used it very well. We can only have respect and admiration for what he has achieved this year.'

Part of Hamilton's achievement had been dealing with the seemingly endless sequence of obstacles. The Fuji race inquiry had been yet another test that he had come through with the same degree of equanimity evident when dealing with everything else that had been thrown at him. While expressing dismay at recent events, Hamilton managed to contain himself and yet indicate that he was not prepared to be trifled with:

> This weekend has been a roller coaster: quite an emotional trip. I arrived nice and early in order to prepare myself but then I found out that I was under investigation. The conditions in Japan had been really difficult but I knew I had done nothing wrong. It felt like being on trial for murder knowing I hadn't done it. Sitting there waiting for the verdict is not a nice thing. I'm like my Dad in that I tend to think the worst on these occasions; I think I'm going to get a penalty. I was very relieved when I was given the all-clear. I felt like I had got rid of a heavy load from my shoulders.

Hamilton continued: 'I just think it's a real shame for the sport. Formula One's supposed to be about hard, fair competition. That's what I've tried to do this year, just be fair. There's been some real strange situations this year where I'm made to look the bad person. If this is the way it's going to keep going it's not somewhere I really want to be.'

Hamilton expressed these views to the media, gathered in one of the permanent buildings constructed in the lavish paddock. Each team had a suite of offices, each on its own island in a man-made lake at the back of the paddock. Interesting and different these might have been but they destroyed the sense of community found in the European paddocks where the teams are parked in close company. Hamilton probably had neither the time nor the inclination to consider the social niceties of the Shanghai paddock but he was to experience at first hand how every branch of F1 had been affected in some way by the split between McLaren and Ferrari.

McLaren were meticulous in allocating time for media interviews. Overseen by Ellen Kolby and her assistant, Claire Barratt, the full complement of international journalists would be given between five and ten minutes with each driver before Alonso would have a further session with the Spanish press, Hamilton doing the same for his fellow compatriots. Hamilton was obviously much in demand following the Fuji inquiry and the British media was looking for a more detailed and exclusive response than the one Lewis had given during the international briefing. It was to be a surprise, therefore, that an Italian journalist should enter the room towards the end of the British audience and pick up a tape recorder that, he claimed, had been accidentally left on the table. It was also an accident, presumably, that the machine was still running.

Hamilton, not realizing the gravity of the situation from a media point of view, looked on in amazement when Ian Gordon, a British journalist, sprang to his feet, shouting 'That's bang out of order, that is, mate!' before berating the Italian in no uncertain terms and demanding that he wipe his recorder clean. Claims of feigned innocence by his European colleague cut no ice with the man from the *News of the World* as the temperature in the room rose dramatically. If the Italian had passed the interview on to an agency in Europe, the exclusive nature of the words from a British media point of view would have been made worthless. Hamilton did not utter a word while all hell broke loose around him.

It was a reminder of how everyone has a job to do and the competitive nature of F1 is not confined to the drivers and their teams. It also cranked up the tension another notch as this championship headed into its final phase. With Hamilton leading Räikkönen by 17 points with just two races to go, the British media appeared to be backing the winner. Who could blame an Italian writer for being bang out of order?

27

Too Fast at 20 m.p.h.

For the first 25 laps, everything seemed perfect. The Chinese Grand Prix had been started on a damp track with all of the leading cars running wet-weather tyres. Hamilton had powered off the line and extended his lead over Räikkönen by about half a second a lap. More important from the championship point of view, Alonso was fourth and falling further behind. At this rate, the title belonged to Hamilton. Then this crazy season took another lurch into the unexpected.

The track had been drying on the racing line but Hamilton had been attempting to look after his tyres by keeping them cool on damper parts of the circuit, even if that meant running off line. There had seemed no cause for alarm when he made his first scheduled stop on lap 15 and the same set of wet-weather tyres remained on the car. Part-worn wet-weather tyres would, in theory, be faster in the greasy conditions than a new set. Certainly, they should have seen Hamilton through to his second and final stop, by which time a change could be made to dry-weather tyres, assuming the forecast was correct in predicting a dry track.

On lap 26, the rain returned. Suddenly, the worn wet-weather tyres were offering no grip at all as the conditions changed from greasy to very slippery in a matter of minutes. Räikkönen should have been in the same predicament but the Finn had not pushed as hard as Hamilton in the early laps and the Ferrari was kinder to its rear tyres, all of which meant Räikkönen's wet-weather rubber was in better condition. Hamilton was powerless to defend his lead as canvas began to show on the rear tyres. The team could see the telltale white strip growing in width with each passing lap. The world at large could also see it. So could the Bridgestone engineers, who urged McLaren to bring Hamilton in for fresh rubber.

But which type of tyre to choose? The McLaren forecast said the rain would soon cease. In which case, dry tyres would be the obvious choice. But what if the forecast was wrong? Alonso's strategy was allowing him to run 3 laps longer, a valuable breathing space that might permit him to make the right choice once the weather had made up its mind. It was immediately obvious that Alonso, rather than Räikkönen, was occupying McLaren's thinking. It was clear evidence that Hamilton was now the de facto number one driver within McLaren. However, focusing on Alonso's actions without thinking of the wider picture would turn out to be a disastrous tactic.

Hamilton was unable to see the state of his rear tyres because his mirrors were dirty. But he knew things were bad thanks to the car handling as if on ice. Having asked to come in, Hamilton had obeyed instructions to stay out a lap longer even though he was being unlapped by Jarno Trulli in fourteenth place: that is how slow the McLaren had become. Meanwhile, Alex Wurz had just set the fastest lap of the race so far. The Williams was on dry-weather tyres. There was the answer. McLaren called Hamilton in at the end of his thirtieth lap.

Having become accustomed to the drying line on the track, Hamilton was caught unawares by the wet entrance to the pit lane. If he felt there had been very little grip beforehand, now he had none at all from rear tyres that were useless. Hamilton had used the narrow pit lane on at least fifteen occasions during the weekend. During that time, he had done his homework as usual by entering as fast as he could in order to discover the levels of grip so as not to lose valuable tenths of a second during pit stops in the race.

He knew all about a ninety-degree left-hand bend not far beyond the entrance. Under normal circumstances, this would be taken at around 25 m.p.h., with no trouble at all. But these were no longer normal circumstances. As Hamilton touched the brakes in preparation for the left-hander, the rear of the McLaren instantly broke away to the right. Hamilton was able to correct the slide, almost without thinking. But there was not enough road to contain the car and allow him to make it through the bend. Before he knew it, Hamilton was heading into the only gravel trap in the world that fringes a pit lane entrance. Quite why the gravel trap should be there did not matter at that precise moment as the McLaren skittered across the top of the stones, but without enough momentum to see it through to the other side. The wheels sank, beaching the flat bottom of the chassis on the wet aggregate. The sanctuary of grass and tarmac lay only a matter of feet beyond the nose of the McLaren.

The world at large, and the McLaren team in particular, could not believe what they were seeing when a television camera suddenly showed the sorry picture as car number 2 sat stationary with its driver urging marshals to push the McLaren to freedom. A couple of seconds of effort by the officials were enough to prove it was a hopeless cause. Hamilton was going nowhere. In the twinkling of an eye, he was out of the race.

After an almost blemish-free season, Hamilton had made a catastrophic error, assisted by his team dithering over what to do about the changeable weather. In fact, the rain had stopped as forecast but, even if Hamilton had been sent out on the wrong tyres, he only needed to finish second to take the title. Such a sequence of elementary misjudgements was yet another extraordinary twist. In a car capable of 200 m.p.h., Hamilton had lost everything at a tenth of that speed.

Chequered Conflict

Hamilton's feet must have felt encased in concrete as he crunched disconsolately through the gravel. Nevertheless, even in the aftermath of such a disaster, he found time on his return to the garage to speak to his mechanics and shake hands with the team management operating at the pit wall before making a quiet departure while the race continued.

Räikkönen, now thoroughly at home at Ferrari, never looked like being challenged by Alonso, whose day had been made when he saw his team-mate's abandoned car at the pit lane entrance. McLaren may have been feeling the pain of having contributed to Hamilton's failure to finish but they could count themselves lucky that it was Hamilton and not Alonso who had come to an embarrassing halt in the gravel. Given Alonso's healthy persecution complex, the Spaniard would have been muttering aloud about conspiracy theories in the belief that the team had deliberately compromised his race in favour of Hamilton.

The paranoia had reached such a pitch that it prompted the FIA to propose the introduction of a steward to oversee fair play in the McLaren garage during the final race in Brazil. Given McLaren's policy of bending over backwards to achieve parity, sometimes to the detriment of the team as a whole, the FIA's unprecedented interference seemed unnecessary. But it was par for the course in a story that had become a travelling soap opera.

Hamilton, meanwhile, could only question his tactics after pressing on in the early stages of the race to the detriment of his tyres when, arguably, there was no need. 'We were clearly in a perfect position to win the championship,' said Hamilton. 'But at the end of the day I wanted to win the race. I was out there driving for the win, and things like that can just happen.'

Hamilton's powerful desire to win had made him such a strong competitor. This time, there had been a price to pay. According to Sir Jackie Stewart, there are critical occasions when natural instinct needs to be curbed, particularly when a driver has a 12-point advantage with two races to go. He said:

Lewis is probably a little bit naive in some respects – as any 22-year-old would be in his first season. He's not thinking as laterally as he will in three or four years' time. He had nothing to prove in the winning department because he'd already won four races, one of which was that superb drive in the rain in Japan. So there comes a time when a driver needs to think: 'Right, now I've got to win the championship', and do whatever that requires at a crucial stage in the season.

Stewart knew what he was talking about, having earned three world titles by adopting the policy of winning races as slowly as possible. Easier said than done, of course. Hamilton had demonstrated the same aggressive attitude as Nigel Mansell although, to be fair to Mansell, an unusually circumspect drive in the final round of the 1986 championship had been denied by the sort of curious misfortune that had visited Hamilton in China twenty-one years later. And both incidents had involved tyres in different but equally dramatic ways.

28

The Slowest Shall
be First

With Nigel Mansell a strong contender for the title, the British media were out in force for the final round of the 1986 championship in Adelaide. This was in stark contrast to the previous year and the inaugural running of the Australian Grand Prix on the streets of this gracious city. In 1985, I had been the sole newspaper reporter representing 'Fleet Street'. With the championship having been concluded, most sports editors considered Australia to be expensive and too distant for their correspondents to travel at the end of a long season. In truth, I would have been absent too were it not for my freelance status bringing in enough extra work, along with my regular commission from the *Guardian*, to pay the bills. It would turn out to be a worthwhile trip.

The welcome was overwhelming, as is often the case at the first running of a Grand Prix. For a street circuit with temporary facilities, the standard was higher than at some permanent tracks in Europe, the extensive garages putting the breezeblock hovels masquerading as pits at Silverstone to shame. The circuit was a perfect mix of angular street corners, a long straight covering the length of Dequetteville Terrace, and an interesting section through the Victoria Park horse-race course, where the pits and paddock were located.

On the second day, I received an ovation on walking into the media centre. My piece in the *Guardian* – which, thankfully, had

been positive in its praise – had been reprinted chapter and ful-
some verse in the *Adelaide Advertiser*. The headline said: 'British
Media Approves of Adelaide'. Which, in a manner of speaking,
was perfectly true. As the unwitting representative of the UK's
national dailies, I thought Adelaide was wonderful – and would
continue to do so until the final race in 1995.

The entire weekend in 1985 was blessed with glorious
weather from start to finish. I naturally assumed these were the
prevailing conditions for the first weekend in November in this
corner of the southern hemisphere, a fact I happily relayed to my
colleagues as they prepared for their first visit twelve months
later. My name would be taken in vain more than once, and usually through chattering teeth. From the moment the F1 circus
arrived in Adelaide in 1986, it would be unseasonably cold. T-
shirts and safari gear were not to be the most appropriate attire.

Calculators were an essential part of the kit. After fifteen races,
Mansell had 70 points, Prost 64 and Piquet 63. However, with
Mansell and Prost having already scored eleven times, they would
have to drop their lowest score (Mansell, 2 points; Prost, 1 point) if
they reached the points once more. Piquet, who had finished in the
top six on ten occasions, was free to take whatever he could without dropping points. This might lead to a situation where Mansell
could lose the championship to a rival who had scored fewer
points in total. An editorial in *Autosport* was not alone in calling for
an end to the 'dropped score' routine and its confusing conse-
quences. The rule had been pushed through in the early days of
turbocharged engines when teams were concerned about the
durability of the turbos; a subsequent improvement in reliability
had rendered the clause superfluous.

As it was, the drivers and teams were having enough trouble
dealing with the limit on fuel capacity and the need to think
about excess consumption rather than simply following the
more natural instinct to race flat out. Keke Rosberg, about to
enter his final Grand Prix before retirement, claimed that the

economy aspect was one of the few things he would not miss. 'It's difficult in the early stages of the race when you're keeping the [turbo] boost low while other drivers are charging into the distance,' said Rosberg. 'You feel such a bloody idiot in those circumstances. You want to scream out to the grandstands, "Hey, I'm not a w*****, you know! I could go a lot faster than this" . . .'

Rosberg's McLaren team-mate had proved adept at staying calm, thinking about the long game and conserving fuel. But, for all that, Prost remained the outsider of the three contenders. In simple terms, if Mansell claimed a place anywhere on the podium, he would be champion regardless of where his rivals finished. Few were betting against the Englishman, particularly when he cleared the first hurdle by winning pole with a lap 0.3 seconds faster than Piquet. Senna set third fastest time with Prost joining the Lotus on the second row. Senna would automatically present Mansell with the title if the Brazilian won the race. Whether Senna would feel so inclined was another question since these two were scarcely close mates, but it was an interesting scenario nonetheless.

Showing commendable restraint after powering off the start line, Mansell moved to one side in order to avoid unnecessary contact as the two Brazilians rushed past, Piquet then taking the lead from Senna at the end of the back straight. Mansell, meanwhile, had dropped another place as Rosberg, the winner of this race twelve months before, showed every intention of leaving F1 with a repeat performance. By lap 7, the Finn was in the lead and pulling away. Prost, having conserved fuel and weighed things up, was beginning his attack as he moved into third, ahead of Mansell. By lap 23, he was second, ahead of Piquet.

This was typical Prost as he found himself ideally placed with 59 laps to run. Rosberg may have been leading – and by quite some distance – but the 1982 world champion had made it clear that he would let Prost win this race if it gave the Frenchman the championship. That suddenly seemed irrelevant when Prost suffered a punctured right-front tyre and made his way slowly to the pits, where it took 17 seconds – a lifetime in F1 terms – to change tyres, the jack man at the front having had difficulty performing his duty because of the lowered state of the car thanks to the punctured tyre. Even though Prost rejoined in fourth place, his championship appeared to have gone the way of the air from his deflated Goodyear. Rosberg continued to lead, with Piquet second. But, significantly, Mansell was holding a comfortable third place and, with it, the championship. Then the picture began to shift, slowly at first, before ending in a powerful drama with Mansell at its centre.

Rosberg had been leading for 63 laps when he heard strange noises from the rear of his McLaren. Assuming the TAG had failed, Rosberg shut down the engine and coasted to a halt by the side of the track. On climbing from the cockpit, Rosberg was surprised to discover that his right-rear tyre had begun to delaminate and it was rubber flailing against the bodywork which had resembled the sound of a V6 ruining its bearings. Rosberg's understandable disappointment over the loss of what would have been an easy victory was later eased by the discovery that one of his brake discs was about to shatter; not the sort of memory he would have wanted of his last race had the failure occurred at the end of the 190 m.p.h. Dequetteville Terrace. Meanwhile, the sole surviving McLaren was truly on the move.

With absolutely nothing to lose, Prost had been driving like a man possessed, setting fastest lap after fastest lap as he moved into second place behind Piquet. But, significantly in terms of the championship, Mansell had been happy to let Prost go since the Williams driver was exactly here he needed to be in third place. Given Mansell's perpetual association with theatre, life had been too straightforward. The Englishman's world was about to explode around his ears.

Powering through the gears on Dequetteville Terrace,

Mansell suddenly felt the left-rear corner of the Williams sit down on its wheel rim. The tyre had failed without warning to send Mansell slewing from side to side, the right-front wheel of the stiffly sprung car pawing the air as he desperately tried to keep control on the wrong side of 175 m.p.h. This being a temporary track, the straight was defined on either side by concrete walls, Mansell somehow managing to avoid them before arriving in the escape road. The Williams finally came to a gentle halt, the left-rear wheel with its tyre now like a long strip of liquorice, giving one final, defiant spasm as Mansell let out the clutch and stalled the engine. If Lewis Hamilton's 2007 season will be forever summed up by the picture of his McLaren beached in a gravel trap in China, then Mansell's 1986 championship will always be remembered for the symbolic picture of thrashing rubber and showering sparks, accompanied by the barely controlled hysteria of Murray Walker as the BBC television commentator roared: 'LOOK AT THAT! It's MANSELL! MANSELL!'

Why had this happened? The plan had been for all of the leading cars to run non-stop, a strategy which had been corroborated by the Goodyear technicians examining Prost's discarded tyres and finding them perfectly capable of finishing the race but for the puncture. However, that did not take into account that the McLaren-TAG was being kinder to its rear tyres than the more powerful Honda engine in the back of the Williams. This seemed to catch everyone by surprise, particularly as Williams had no intention of taking even the slightest chance. Patrick Head, the Williams technical director, was very unhappy with this latest development and the implications for Piquet's leading car: 'At no time were we considering taking any sort of gamble. After all, we were in a position where we had to play things safe and conservatively. I don't blame Goodyear for the fact that it happened but they gave us absolutely no reason to consider we needed to change tyres. That tyre did not explode because it was worn out.

Chequered Conflict

The bits of tyre that were recovered indicated that the carcass had failed, by fatigue.'

Head went on: 'In fact, Nigel had been in a position where he could have stopped for tyres and still gone on to get the championship because there was no one close behind him. I had told a Goodyear engineer that we had time to do that, but he said that we should have no problem; from the tyre wear they had measured, it seemed to be perfectly okay.'

Now the Williams team had a dilemma. Piquet was continuing to lead and, with Mansell's disappearance, the Brazilian was perfectly poised to take the title. But Prost was only a couple of seconds behind. Both drivers needed the 9 points that came with victory in order to become world champion.

'We were between a rock and a hard place,' said Head. 'If we'd have left him out there and he'd made it, we'd have looked like heroes. But if he'd had an accident and hurt himself, we'd have looked like idiots. There was no choice, in fact. We called him in and changed his tyres.'

Piquet stopped at the end of lap 64. He rejoined in second place. Prost appeared to have it made. But the drama was not yet over.

For quite some time the on-board fuel readout had been informing Prost that he was 5 litres on the wrong side. But the Frenchman, knowing that Piquet was closing rapidly thanks to the benefit of fresh tyres, pressed on in the knowledge that he may as well. Second place would be of no use to Prost. If the car ran out of fuel, then so be it; he would have lost the championship.

With the McLaren in sight, Piquet set yet another record on the final lap. Prost's heart was in his mouth as he entered Victoria Park and headed for the final hairpin for the eighty-second time. Miraculously, the TAG engine kept running as he accelerated on to the finish straight to win the championship, the first time a driver had done so in successive years since Jack Brabham in

1959/60. Prost pulled over immediately, climbed from the cockpit, the little man jumping for joy. He could scarcely believe it. Neither, for that matter, could Williams. Their car had unquestionably been the fastest and yet they had lost.

The British media's search for Mansell ended when they found him trying to make a quiet exit. Dressed in jeans and a leather flying jacket with a fleece collar, Mansell was gradually pinned against the wire mesh fence surrounding the fuel store at the back of the paddock. As he expressed his obvious disappointment, there was little more that anyone could add. This had been the most dramatic race many of us had seen, greatly enhanced by on-board shots from the Lotus of Johnny Dumfries, the first footage of its kind in F1. Yet, standing quietly and without ceremony with Mansell on that chilly afternoon, it seemed a strange way for the Englishman's long and colourful championship campaign to reach its conclusion. All three contenders had been, at various stages in the race, in a position to win the title. Mansell and Piquet had been fighting it out all year and Prost, in a red and white car, had managed to motor through the middle. That scenario would have a familiar resonance twenty-one years later.

29

Gone in an Instant

People talked about the last time three contenders had gone into the final round of the world championship, but it meant little to Lewis Hamilton. He was one year old when Nigel Mansell made his spectacular exit from the 1986 Australian Grand Prix. Now Hamilton was heading for Brazil in an attempt to become the seventh Englishman to win the title.

Despite the slightly crumbling and chaotic nature of the Interlagos track, Hamilton liked it straight away. This was where Ayrton Senna had been revered and Hamilton somehow felt closer to his hero. But it was a sign of the youngster's rocketing status that an attempt to make a quiet visit to Senna's grave at the nearby Morumbi cemetery had to be abandoned because of the paparazzi's constant presence wherever Hamilton went. Felipe Massa would be the new home hero, of course, but Hamilton was already big in Brazil and clearly favoured by the locals over Alonso.

At least the Spaniard had the support of the FIA as a steward was positioned in the McLaren garage to ensure fair play after Alonso's complaints about tyre pressures in China. In the end, even Alonso agreed that it was unnecessary. As for the team, Ron Dennis made it clear that McLaren had no objection to officials doing what-ever they wished in his garage because the team had nothing to hide. Dennis explained just how Alonso had been slower during qualifying in Shanghai, the cause of the Spaniard's displeasure.

Chequered Conflict

'Part of the difference in lap time was because Lewis had a lower level of fuel and he made up time on Fernando in two specific braking areas, one in which he picked up nearly two tenths of a second,' said Dennis. 'So the difference in lap time was fuel load and specific points on the circuit where Lewis did a very good job on braking. Those are the absolute facts and maybe not what Fernando felt when he got out of the car.' In the light of Dennis's previous and sometimes pathetic efforts not to offend Alonso, this amounted to rampant criticism of the double world champion.

Anyone hoping for sparks to fly at the FIA press conference was to be disappointed when the three contenders took to the stage. The McLaren drivers seemed relaxed in each other's company: Räikkönen looked the same as ever; bemused and slightly bored. Of the three, Räikkönen was in the best position because the mathematics dictated that he simply had to win the race; anything less and the title would go to a McLaren driver. That suited Räikkönen fine. Hamilton, although 4 points clear of Alonso, had the more difficult task of finding the right balance between pushing hard but without taking unnecessary risks. Even so, the best way to start would be by claiming pole. But, to do that, Hamilton would probably need to deal with Massa, the winner of the previous year's race and the one driver who could be a thorn in Hamilton's side. With his championship chance having disappeared, Massa would be out to provide legitimate help for Räikkönen. It was a potential problem that did not seem to bother Hamilton when the subject was raised:

I've not really thought about that, to be honest. In the last few races, Kimi's been the one that made the charge for the title but, because he was quite far behind in points, Felipe's not really been a major threat. He'll be going out there to do his own job and I think perhaps, if the team ask him, maybe he will try and get in the way. Even if Kimi's in the lead and

Felipe's behind him and holding me up, that's not really a big problem for me. I'll only need to finish fifth, so it's not a big issue.

The important thing is that I'm comfortable with the pace of my car, and with my abilities. And I have no doubt that we can do a better job than them. I'm not going to be thinking, 'Shit, I've gotta watch out for Felipe.' I'm out there to beat them all. I think we still have to approach the race weekend by trying to take pole position, lead from the start and win the race.

He added thoughtfully, as if referring to the shambles in China, 'But I think some part of the mind has to be focused on the end result.'

Once the conference had finished, an attempt to have the three contenders photographed together failed. This was no surprise to Roger Benoit, the Swiss journalist who had set up a photograph of Senna, Mansell, Piquet and Prost on the pit wall in Portugal in 1986. Benoit tried to repeat the process in 2007 but Ferrari refused to allow Räikkönen to take part. When no satisfactory reason was given, this was seen as a sad reflection of the hard-nosed attitudes of the day and did little for either Ferrari's curmudgeonly image or the sometimes unnecessary friction in the paddock.

After rain during the first day of practice, conditions were perfect on Saturday. When the crunch came in the third and final part of qualifying, Massa was the first to set a quick time and claim provisional pole. Räikkönen was next but the start of his fast lap coincided with Hamilton emerging from the pits on his out lap. The pit lane exit at Interlagos fed cars on to the straight leading towards a left-hander at turn 4, Subida do Lago. Räikkönen noted the McLaren ahead on the left, but he could not be completely sure that Hamilton had seen the Ferrari. After veering slightly towards the centre of the track, Hamilton stayed off the racing line, but the momentary distraction was enough to disturb Räikkönen's flow as he turned into the 140-m.p.h. corner. The Ferrari went into a brief slide, enough to ensure that Räikkönen was 0.24 seconds slower than Massa. Hamilton duly took his turn and claimed second fastest time to split Massa and Räikkönen. Given that the Ferraris were marginally better suited to Interlagos, Hamilton had done all that could be reasonably expected.

'It was really close,' said Hamilton. 'I really enjoyed the session. The car was nice to drive; it was a really good lap. It was quite straightforward. I lost a bit of time in the last corner, not because of a mistake but because I didn't want to spoil the lap right at the end. I'm just buzzing, feeling really excited. The car feels great and I love the circuit. I feel very relaxed and it was good to see quite a few British flags out there. I appreciate the support.'

There was little support coming from a section of the interview room when the subject of Räikkönen's fast lap was raised during the post-qualifying press conference. Hamilton explained that he had been told by radio of Räikkönen's presence but found it difficult to judge his approach speed.

'I couldn't tell just how close he was,' said Hamilton. 'I stayed where I was, backed off and he went past me. I don't feel that I hindered his lap. I apologized afterwards in case I had caused a problem. I just need to do a completely clean job this weekend. If anything, Kimi could win this race and that would be good for me in terms of the championship because my first priority is to beat Fernando.'

Räikkönen was his usual phlegmatic self when discussing the incident. 'I don't know how much time I lost,' said Räikkönen. 'For sure he could have found a slightly easier way to let me past but what's happened has happened.'

That was not enough for Anne Giuntini. The motor sport correspondent for *L'Equipe* pursued a line of questioning that became so aggressive that Hamilton, looking slightly startled, said he no longer wished to speak to the Frenchwoman. Undeterred, Giuntini later tried to take the matter up with Ron Dennis and Anthony Hamilton. She received little time or sympathy from either. Just as predictable, Ferrari took the matter to the stewards, raising the possibility of a penalty for Hamilton. The stewards were of the view that this had been a straightforward incident and no action would be taken.

Giuntini's uncharacteristic outburst was the first public sign of a potential backlash against Hamilton's performances and the threat of Schumacher-style domination in the years to come. It simply added another turn of the screw, as did England losing the final of the rugby world cup, the nation then turning its attention from Paris to Brazil in the hope that Hamilton could move Britain out of the seemingly permanent role of also-ran: or loser, depending on the degree of pessimism.

Massa, the only leading contender with nothing to lose, was enjoying his second successive pole position at home. 'It's a fantastic feeling,' said the Brazilian. 'I made a mistake and I was afraid Lewis could beat me. It was very close and I was expecting to hear I was second, but I had done enough. The reaction of the crowd was fantastic. I'm in front and I'm sure the team is happy with me. We'll see what happens in the race.'

One of the few positive points to emerge from Hamilton's retirement in China had been the knowledge that the championship would be settled at one of the oldest and most charismatic venues on the F1 calendar. Perched on an escarpment, Interlagos is 750 metres above sea level. At the time of track's inauguration in 1940, the view of São Paulo in the distance clearly showed Congonhas but the local airport is now lost within the urban sprawl that has engulfed Interlagos, thus adding further ambience to a track that may be shabby in parts but which has always been loved for its challenge and character.

When Interlagos staged a round of the championship for the

first time in 1973, the track measured 4.9 miles as it twisted and turned spectacularly within itself. Unable to pay the price of incorporating the necessary safety standards, the owners cut the circuit length in half during a ten-year absence from the F1 calendar. When the Brazilian Grand Prix returned from a period at Rio de Janeiro, the drivers were delighted and relieved to find that the essential flavour of Interlagos remained. Named after a Brazilian F1 hero killed in a plane crash in 1977, the Autódromo José Carlos Pace stands out as a proper place to go motor racing in a series increasingly populated by immaculate but bland facilities.

The pits may be ancient and cramped but the view from the back of the paddock, on the highest part of the track, sums up the appeal. Interlagos comprises a devious infield section on the valley floor and a long, fast climb to the main straight before plunging left and downhill at the first corner. Setting up a F1 car to meet the disparate requirements of this track could be as tricky as actually tackling it. While a driver wanted aerodynamic downforce to provide grip and traction in the tight corners, the wings necessary to achieve that would be a major hindrance in the quest to reach 185 m.p.h. at the end of 17 seconds of flat-out driving on the top straight. A shortfall in performance here would leave a driver vulnerable to an overtaking move when approaching the braking area for the first corner.

The track had been resurfaced. While that may have removed some of the notoriously difficult bumps, the fresh asphalt was creating unforeseen problems with tyre wear. With the track temperature during qualifying reaching 57 degrees C, the highest in 2007, drivers were struggling to avoid excessive wear on the softer of the two types of tyre, both of which had to be used during the 71-lap race. All told, it seemed to favour Ferrari.

The red cars would be starting from the clean side of the track. Hamilton knew this could be tricky. Sure enough, the Ferrari drivers boxed him beautifully, Massa legitimately moving in front of the McLaren and holding Hamilton back just enough to allow Räikkönen alongside and into second place. As the field swung through the first corner and downhill towards the second, Räikkönen checked a brief slide. Seeing a chance to retaliate, Hamilton closed up on the Ferrari. Realizing he might be vulnerable to attack, Räikkönen used the oldest trick in the book by backing off the throttle for barely a second, but just enough to cause Hamilton to do the same. That momentary hesitation was all Alonso needed to draw alongside on his team-mate's left and push Hamilton down to fourth place. Hamilton might have been able to live with Räikkönen's tactics but having Alonso move in front was too much to take.

In a season noted for his coolness under pressure, Hamilton momentarily lost reason and tried an over-ambitious move as the McLarens sped down the back straight towards turn 4. Alonso saw him coming. Second-guessing his team-mate, Alonso stayed in the middle of the road, forcing Hamilton to attempt a run round the outside. It ended with Hamilton overshooting the corner and dropping to eighth place as he recovered in the dusty run-off area. It was the first time Hamilton had been suckered like a novice. But all was not lost because he merely needed to move into fifth place to keep the championship lead that he had held since Bahrain in April. Then his luck really turned sour.

Having gone for sixteen races without a mechanical failure, Hamilton's gearbox chose lap 8 of the final Grand Prix to select neutral without warning. The McLaren telemetry told the engineers that the electronics controlling the gearbox hydraulics had suffered a glitch. It would be necessary for Hamilton to reboot the system. The process of flicking the gear selection paddles and pushing buttons on the steering wheel in a certain sequence took about twenty seconds, during which time Hamilton suffered the additional frustration of watching most of the field sweep past. By the time the electronics had been reset, Hamilton had dropped to eighteenth place. There was no option but to start all over again and see where he finished.

The team, meanwhile, were examining the strategic options presented by this unexpected turn of events. Hamilton's engineers knew that he would need to use both types of tyre. They also knew that the softer of the two would not last long on the hot track surface. A plan was hatched to use these tyres for the minimum amount of time during the middle stint. When Hamilton made his first pit stop at the end of lap 22, a small amount of fuel was duly added and the soft tyres fitted. Hamilton was quickly under way, rejoining in fifteenth place as he started a run of 14 laps. It was then that the McLaren team realized their plan would never work.

Examination of the discarded harder tyres showed the Bridgestones to be almost worn out after just 22 laps. The similar tyres set aside for the final stint would never last the 35 laps required by the revised strategy. Hamilton would have to make yet another stop for fresh rubber, in the process losing around thirty seconds – and any hope of winning the championship.

Ferrari, meanwhile, were running the perfect race. Massa led until his second stop when a judicious strategy saw Räikkönen move into the lead and head for the victory that would give him the title as Alonso finished a distant third and Hamilton came home seventh, 2 points short of the total needed become champion. Hamilton said:

Obviously, I'm pretty disappointed with the result today, having led for so much of the season and then not to win the championship. However, I have to put the result into perspective. This is only my first year of F1 and overall it has just been phenomenal. I'm still very young and have plenty more years in me to achieve my dream of becoming world champion. I have to thank absolutely everyone in the team for everything they have done for me this year. And I also want to pay my respects to Kimi. He's a great guy and he deserves this championship; I'm genuinely pleased for him.

Hamilton had nothing to be ashamed of. He had set new standards, far beyond anything even his most ardent admirer could have predicted before the start of the season. Hamilton had finished on the podium in nine successive races, gone on to win four Grands Prix and led the championship most of the way. No other novice in the history of the sport had even come close. It was true that Hamilton had a competitive car at his disposal but it was the manner in which he had used it that set the youngster apart. The performance of a chastened Alonso gave witness to that. Even in moments of defeat, Hamilton had maintained a dignity and maturity that was unique and indicated that an easy confidence created by such outstanding natural ability heralded the arrival of a special talent. It had been a tough fight and Hamilton's recognition of the new world champion's achievement was genuine and well founded.

Räikkönen was grinning from ear to ear. This result was made even sweeter after such a difficult start to his first year with Ferrari. In the end, Räikkönen thoroughly deserved the title, if only because he had won two more races than anyone else.

Three hours after the finish, and having dealt with the interviews and formalities, Räikkönen hurried away from the paddock. Dressed in beige shorts and a T-shirt with a Ferrari rucksack on his back, the Finn and two friends quickly descended an iron staircase and walked briskly into an almost deserted car park where his silver Fiat Stilo was waiting. A race fan, who happened to be passing, could hardly believe his luck as he got the autograph of the 2007 world champion. Or so he thought. High above them in the paddock offices, a FIA technical delegate was gathering some worrying news. This extraordinary story was not yet at an end.

30

The Fat Lady Sings
Out of Tune

Seven hours after the finish in Brazil, the identity of the 2007 world champion remained unknown. There could have been no better summary of this bizarre season than that. Kimi Räikkönen had left Interlagos in the belief that his sixth win for Ferrari had been enough to claim the title by a single point. But, as he headed into downtown São Paulo, the race stewards were pondering a report from Jo Bauer, the F1 technical delegate. The officials were discussing the temperature of fuel samples taken from a Williams and two BMWs that had finished fourth, fifth and sixth. This was significant because, if all three were excluded, then Lewis Hamilton would move from seventh to fourth place – and win the championship.

Fuel in F1 could be cooled, but only to a maximum of 10 degrees below the ambient temperature. The samples taken from the Williams and BMWs were found to exceed the limit by a couple of degrees. At 10 p.m., the stewards decided there was too much doubt over how the ambient temperature should be measured and declared that the results would stand. It seemed a spurious excuse. But that was the end of the story – for the time being. Räikkönen remained world champion but McLaren announced their intention to lodge an appeal against the stewards' decision.

A world championship that had exploded regularly almost from the start in Australia on 18 March finally went out with a whimper on a chilly night in London on 16 November. That was when the FIA issued a brief statement to say that McLaren's appeal had been thrown out. Or 'declared inadmissible', to use the legal jargon. It had taken all day for the appeal court judges to reach that decision.

Cynics, of whom there were many after such a contentious season, said the FIA had waited that long in order to have the news make a minimal impact in the media, this being a Friday night and editors would have lost interest thanks to other sports stories taking precedence as the weekend began to unfold.

The underlying element was that the Brazilian results stood. Nobody, least of all McLaren and Hamilton, wished to see the championship won by default. Nevertheless, McLaren had felt the stewards were wrong in rejecting the technical delegate's report and they were dissatisfied with the outcome of the appeal court. Immediately after the verdict Martin Whitmarsh said:

We have not yet seen the text of the FIA International Court of Appeal decision. It's important to stress that the FIA stewards' inquiry at the Brazilian Grand Prix was not triggered by any action from McLaren, but by a report written and made public by the FIA technical delegate, which drew the FIA stewards' attention to what we regarded as a clear regulation breach on the part of BMW-Sauber and Williams. Our appeal was merely a logical and procedural step in the process begun by the FIA technical delegate's written report. We hope that this fuel temperature issue does not remain unresolved in Formula One next year but we look forward to working with the FIA and the teams on clarifying matters to avoid a similar situation occurring again.

The FIA had removed themselves – and their championship – from a potentially painful hook by pointing out that McLaren had followed the incorrect procedure. Instead of lodging an appeal against the results of the Brazilian Grand Prix, McLaren had submitted an appeal against a race stewards' decision that did not directly concern McLaren. Only those intimately involved – in this case, BMW and Williams – were permitted to petition the decision. The fact that McLaren's appeal had been accepted after the race by the chief steward appeared to be irrelevant. Furthermore, the FIA noted that McLaren should have protested the results within thirty minutes of them becoming official.

Either way, the Court of Appeal verdict had allowed the FIA to neatly sidestep the awkward prospect of either their technical delegate having measured the fuel temperature incorrectly or the rules themselves being ambiguous. McLaren – and F1 as a whole – were no closer to finding out exactly how the post-race discrepancy had arisen.

The FIA had also done F1 no favours by having the Court of Appeal take thirty-six hours to decide that McLaren's appeal was not admissible. There had been an hour of argument about this very subject at the beginning of the hearing. Then the case went ahead, evidence was produced by all of the parties involved – only to have the court say eventually that this had more or less been a waste of time. It was curious behaviour from a ruling body that tended to be touchy about criticism of its methods of governance.

Whatever the background to the decision, the results stood and Räikkönen was the 2007 world champion. Nothing would change that. But there were to be two more revelations, one of which would wound McLaren's pride even more than the failure to win either championship.

31
McLaren Destroyed

Considering the turmoil that had followed McLaren every step of the way during 2007, the team's lavish headquarters in Woking was an oasis of calm on 9 November when other parts of F1 seemed ready to implode. Yet another spy scandal had rocked the sport. The irony was that, in this instance, McLaren were named as the aggrieved party after key pieces of their engineering information were found to have been in Renault's possession. Details of Renault's alleged transgression were made public by the FIA and Ron Dennis would not have been alone in musing over the size of the rod that the sport's governing body appeared to have made for its own back.

McLaren's reputation and bank balance remained numbed and depleted thanks to the beating delivered by the FIA in September. The stripping of championship points and imposition of a $100-million fine had set a hefty precedent that looked like proving difficult for the FIA to follow since, on paper, Renault's alleged crime appeared equally serious.

The FIA statement claimed that Renault had in their possession the layout and critical dimensions of the McLaren F1 car, together with details of the McLaren fuelling system, gear assembly, oil cooling system, hydraulic control system and a novel suspension component. Renault explained that a former McLaren engineer, Phil Mackereth, brought the information on floppy disks when he switched teams in 2006.

Chequered Conflict

A Renault statement said:

This information was loaded at the request of Mr Mackereth onto his personal directory on the Renault F1 Team file system. This was done without the knowledge of anyone in authority in the team. Mr Mackereth was immediately suspended from his position. Subsequent witness statements from the engineers involved have categorically stated that having been briefly shown these drawings, none of this information was used to influence design decisions relating to the Renault car.

That was almost a carbon copy of the statements emanating from McLaren earlier in the year when discussing the receipt of information from Ferrari by their former chief designer. None of the Ferrari information was found on McLaren's computers. If McLaren were punished so heavily on the suspicion that Ferrari information may have been used, then it was felt that the penalty due to Renault should be similar. In which case, the Anglo-French team's 2007 world championship results might be in question regardless of Renault's claim that their case was one specific incident whereas McLaren were involved in the constant dripping of information from Ferrari.

Whatever the verdict, this latest revelation, along with the McLaren–Ferrari spy scandal, had emphasized a new dimension to the age-old problem of employees moving from one team to another and taking valuable information with them. Formerly, those sensitive details may have been in the engineer's head but the substitution of computer disks or, in the case of Ferrari and McLaren, a 780-page document had changed the complexion entirely. The hearing in Monaco on 6 December was awaited with interest. In the meantime, McLaren would instigate a sequence of events that would contribute to their downfall, and not that of Renault.

McLaren leaked information concerning the extent of Renault's alleged crime, details that were remarkably similar to the facts surrounding their transgression with Ferrari. This uncharacteristic action backfired dramatically when, on the eve of the WMSC hearing, McLaren were forced reveal that their unofficial briefing had been wholly inaccurate. The briefing, which was widely reported, revolved around the extent to which the McLaren information had permeated inside the Renault team. A statement from McLaren said:

The FIA has asked us to correct certain factual errors contained in a press briefing given on our behalf by one journalist concerning Renault F1 and we are pleased to do so. The corrections are as follows.

In our briefing, we stated that there were 18 witness statements from Renault employees admitting that they had viewed McLaren confidential information.

To the extent that this implied that 18 different Renault employees admitted viewing McLaren confidential information it was inaccurate. 13 Renault F1 employees provided 18 witness statements and nine of them have so far admitted they viewed and discussed the confidential technical information belonging to McLaren.

We stated that the confidential information on computer disks was uploaded onto 11 Renault computers.

This is not accurate. Mr Mackereth copied information onto 11 computer disks. The information on these 11 computer disks was uploaded by Renault IT staff in September 2006 onto Renault's drive and then transferred by Mr Mackereth to his personal home directory stored on Renault's network server. A back up copy of the material on Mr Mackereth's personal directory was made onto an unknown number of Renault's back up servers/tapes.

Our briefing could have been interpreted as suggesting

that the Renault employees who admitted sight of McLaren Confidential Information all viewed it on computer screens.

Only Mr Mackereth and Mr Hardie admit viewing McLaren Confidential Information on Mr Mackereth's computer. The other seven employees who have admitted seeing McLaren Confidential Information admit seeing it in the form of computer print outs or hard copy documents.

We said that the information on the 11 computer disks taken by Mr Mackereth included 780 individual drawings.

This was an error. The information taken by Mr Mackereth on floppy disks, in hard copy form and by email amounts to 762 pages when printed out. The 11 computer disks included 18 individual technical drawings. Mr Mackereth also admits that he took hard copy drawings of McLaren's dampers.

We said that the McLaren information amounted to the 'entire technical blueprint of the 2006 and 2007 McLaren car'.

This requires clarification. The position is that, the McLaren drawings plus the information in a confidential MP4-22A Specification document taken by Mr Mackereth constitute a technical definition of the fundamental layout of the 2007 McLaren car and the technical details of its innovative and performance enhancing systems.

We are pleased to assist the FIA in making the above clear in advance of tomorrow's hearing.

This was a hugely embarrassing climbdown for McLaren – and it would not be the last. But, first, the WMSC had to reach its verdict.

Renault were found to have breached the regulations but, because this revolved around just four of McLaren's drawings, Renault escaped without punishment. McLaren were not alone in being stunned by the judgement. An apparent effort to provide transparency into the sport's inner workings has actually caused confusion in the mind of the casual observer. Despite an elaborate explanation by the WMSC of an examination into alleged impropriety by Renault, it was difficult to fathom why the Anglo-French team had not been given a harsh punishment similar to that served on McLaren. Renault had admitted to a former McLaren employee loading thirty-three files of McLaren technical data onto the Renault system, something that was never proven at McLaren in relation to the Ferrari case.

There were, according to the WMSC, important differences between the two cases. Their statement said:

> The WMSC has concluded that of the four drawings actually viewed by Renault's engineers, three were either of no use to Renault or were not in fact used by Renault. The fourth drawing [a drawing of McLaren's so-called 'J-damper'] was used by Renault in that Renault admits taking it into account in preparing a request to the FIA for a clarification of whether a particular hypothetical system was within the rules [rather than for the purposes of copying it].
>
> The fact that Renault fundamentally misunderstood the operation of the system suggests that the 'J-damper' drawing did not reveal to Renault enough about the system for the championship to have been affected.

Whichever way you looked at the technical jargon, it was difficult to make those variations add up to $100 million, a penalty that now seemed even more ludicrous than before. Max Mosley continued to insist that McLaren had been cheating. In an interview with Richard Williams, published in the *Guardian*, Mosley explained the difference between the Renault and McLaren cases:

> In the case of Renault every single document and interview was sent to us, right from the beginning, in contrast to

McLaren, where there was just a blank denial. And when all the dust settled, there were four drawings, that's all. There was no other evidence. The Renault case bears no relation at all to the McLaren case. But by carefully spinning it – well, actually, lying about it – they [McLaren] created the perception that it did.

Nonetheless, that did not answer the charge that Renault had been in possession of material belonging to another team, a point which had been raised by Flavio Briatore when the managing director of Renault F1 had commented on McLaren escaping sanction in exactly the same way after the initial WMSC hearing. 'I don't understand what happened,' Briatore had said in July. 'If the FIA admits to having established possession of Ferrari material by McLaren, then why is there no retribution?'

An interesting question, but one that Briatore seemed keen to avoid repeating on 6 December.

Adding further spice to the occasion, the WMSC agreed to the FIA suing the *Sunday Times* and their columnist Martin Brundle. Furthermore, the sport's governing body also announced that a report investigating possible Ferrari input into next year's McLaren would not be discussed further until 14 February. McLaren therefore faced the prospect of waiting until four weeks before the start of the 2008 season before learning whether or not their car had been approved. Meanwhile, neither Brundle nor the *Sunday Times* were going to take this lying down. In his column the following Sunday (9 December), the ITV commentator wrote:

As a former Formula One driver, I have earnt the right to have an opinion about the sport, and probably know as much about it as anybody else. I have attended approaching 400 Grands Prix, 158 as a driver. I have spilt blood, broken bones, shed tears, generated tanker loads of sweat, tasted the champagne glories and plumbed the depths of misery. I have never been more passionate about F1 and will always share my opinions in an honest and open way, knowing readers will make up their own minds.

The timing of the writ [against the *Sunday Times*] is significant, in my view, given the FIA's decision to find Renault guilty of having significant McLaren designs and information within their systems, but not administering any penalty. It is a warning sign to other journalists and publications to choose their words carefully over that decision. I'm tired of what I perceive as the 'spin' and tactics of the FIA press office, as are many other journalists. I expect my accreditation pass for next year will be hindered in some way to make my coverage of F1 more difficult and to punish me. Or they will write to ITV again to say that my commentary is not up to standard despite my unprecedented six Royal Television Society Awards for sports broadcasting. So be it.

This past couple of weeks I have attended many functions where I have met high-level F1 people, among many others. The discussion always moves to 'how will the FIA get themselves out of this corner by not punishing Renault despite the outcome of the McLaren case'. That was the perception of many, and remains the billion-dollar question.

I have no issue with Renault or McLaren, they are both former teams of mine and I remain good friends with many in the teams and admire all they have achieved. But very few drivers or key team personnel in F1 can look you in the eye and honestly say they have never witnessed or been part of a transfer of information between teams. The purpose of poaching other team players is to fast-track the development and performance of the car. It's a question of where the line is drawn about transfer of knowledge and intellectual property.

The immensely successful former F1 designer Gordon Murray made a good point when he said that years ago it would have taken several vans to carry the paper-based designs from one team to another. With the digital age and the massively increased complexity of today's cars, along with the pressure created by the billions of dollars of funding from the manufacturers and sponsors, the stakes have changed and the line needs clarifying. Of course the FIA and any legal system engaged in the process are right to investigate this.

Many drivers and team bosses will be mighty relieved they haven't been dragged into this. The guillotine fell as McLaren went under it and Renault have passed unscathed. It is enlightening to read the transcripts from the separate cases. The McLaren judgement is about negativity and suspicion of possible use of Ferrari information, but no real show-stopper I could see. Even now the decision to punish or exclude McLaren for 2008 has been deferred.

The Renault decision is one of an understanding and supportive nature and one only of occasional 'strong disapproval' despite clear and confirmed evidence that information was loaded on to their mainframe IT system, including drawings of McLaren's shock absorber, fuel system, mass damper and seamless shift transmission. Some drawings were printed off and idly laid on a key desk before being handed back after a disinterested glance, said the verdict. I laughed out loud on that one. And just as McLaren protested Ferrari's floor back at the Australian Grand Prix, Renault used information taken from a McLaren 'J-Damper' drawing to seek rule clarification with the FIA. It was deemed that, as with McLaren, it could not be proven Renault benefited from it. Surprisingly, although the case is left open if further information surfaces, unlike McLaren, the Renault team will not be investigated with regard to their 2008 car. Why would that be? I accept there was an element of 'live' transfer of unpublished information over three months between Stepney of Ferrari and Coughlan of McLaren, but it seems the actual proof of information within the Renault team was significantly more damning.

This issue badly needs clearing up, but the Renault verdict muddies the water. All teams now know the ground rules have changed a lot. To an extent Ferrari, McLaren and Renault are all culpable for being careless with their systems and personnel with regard to the security and transfer in and out of their critical designs and operating procedures. How that many people and that much information can be defined and controlled is another matter. It seems like a good memory might be a strong quality for future designers.

In the light of what was about to happen – the final, astonishing act of 2007 – the ability to understand and manage your workforce might also be a strong quality for future team principals. On 13 December, McLaren issued a statement which stunned everyone in F1, not least many of the team's employees. It was admitted by McLaren that their 2008 car did indeed have Ferrari influence within its design and structure. It was impossible not to recall the words of an emotional Ron Dennis when news of the Ferrari scandal first broke at Silverstone in July:

I live and breathe this team. There is no way anything incorrect would ever happen in our team ... My personal integrity is very important to me and my company's integrity is even more important to me. We are working closely with the FIA and closely with Ferrari. This matter does not involve our company ... I am absolutely confident that with the passing of time, the world will understand that McLaren's position is one that is reflective of our statements. We have never, to my knowledge, ever used other people's intellectual property. It is not on our car. I am sure the FIA

will confirm that either now or in the future, and that is the
key message.

Those words had come back to haunt Dennis in the worst possible way. What amounted to a grovelling apology on 13
December had revealed the full extent of infiltration of Ferrari
information onto not only the car which had won eight races in
2007 but also on to the MP4/23, the model under construction
for 2008. It was perfectly clear that Dennis had no idea of the
extent of the penetration of Ferrari technicalities within his
team but that, in turn, pointed to serious weaknesses within
his management. The integrity of a team, previously noted for
its immaculate and unimpeachable image, had been ripped apart
by the actions of engineers dealing with information leaked
by a disaffected Ferrari employee. Dennis had been planning
to gradually relinquish control of the company he had run with
varying success for twenty-five years. It was felt within F1 circles
that this latest revelation might hasten his departure.

Although neither McLaren nor the FIA would admit as much,
such a move looked like being part of a plea bargain which had
prompted the sport's governing body, hours after the publication
of the apology, to suddenly bring the scandal to an end by can-
celling the inspection of the 2008 McLaren on 14 February.
McLaren had been caught between a rock and a hard place
because any revelations discovered just four weeks before the
first race in Melbourne would have wrecked their season and
compromised the chances of Hamilton and his new team-mate,
Heikki Kovalainen.

Either Dennis knew about the full extent of the Ferrari per-
meation within his company or he was in ignorance of the
corrosive actions of a handful of his employees. There was
nothing to show that he knew and it was probably the latter
but, even so, such poor administration and control, if not by Dennis
then by his lieutenants, exacerbated management mistakes which

had contributed to Hamilton's failure to win a championship which had been within his grasp two races from the end of the season.

It could be argued that the £200 million McLaren headquarters had been another of Dennis's misjudgements. The building may have been stunning in appearance but its essential core – the workforce – had found difficulty feeling at home despite such elegant surroundings. A racing team needs to work cheek by jowl and think on its feet. The vast, impersonal nature of the McLaren facility had been highlighted by the right hand clearly being unaware of what the left hand had been doing.

Many McLaren employees, rightly believing all they had been told by Dennis, were as shocked as the outside world by the nature and scope of the damage. The workforce had laboured tirelessly throughout the season, producing over 3000 modifications to the MP4/22. Losing both championships had been bad enough; hearing news such as this was devastating.

The revelation of wrongdoing had, to a degree, justified the FIA's merciless pummelling of McLaren. But far greater harm had been inflicted on the morale of a team that had the world at its feet until the first indication of the spying drama in July. McLaren's ability to regroup and fight back in 2008 would be the greatest test ever faced by a team with a once proud record.

Typically, Ferrari were not content to let the matter rest. A pre-Christmas press briefing allowed Jean Todt and Ferrari's president, Luca di Montezemolo, to issue statements of continuing outrage over the absence of a 100 per cent guilty verdict in September. McLaren's admission of culpability had played into Ferrari's hands but, for those who wished to see closure, the protests from Italy were neither welcome nor appropriate for a team that had been involved in its share of controversy over the years.

Bending the rules and searching for the unfair advantage have always been part of the game, and will continue to be the case for any team with a rage to win. Ferrari had deservedly won both championships. However, this was the time neither to crow nor to criticize. The 2007 season had been one of the most engaging, thrilling and momentous in the history of the sport. Now it was at a close. The smiling faces and comradeship of the McLaren drivers on the beach in Melbourne seemed from another time. In some respects, F1 had changed irrevocably in the intervening nine months, never mind in the preceding twenty-one years. In other ways, it had not changed at all.

ACKNOWLEDGEMENTS

I am grateful to the following media organisations for reference material:

Autocourse, *Autosport*, Autosport.com, BBC Radio 5 Live, *F1 Racing*, Grand Prix.com, *Observer Sport Monthly*, the *Adelaide Advertiser*, the *Daily Mail*, the *Daily Telegraph*, the FIA, the *Guardian*, the *Observer*, the *Red Bulletin*, the *Sunday Times*, *The Times*.

Thanks, also, to my colleagues and friends for their company, 'craic' and (sometimes unwitting) contributions during this extraordinary journey: Simon Arron, Alan Baldwin, Claire Barrett, Matt Bishop, Ann Bradshaw, Martin Brundle, Luca Colajanni, Tim Collings, Bob Constanduros, Steve Cooper, David Croft, Tony Dodgins, Kevin Garside, Louise Goodman, Ian Gordon, Ed Gorman, Alan Henry, Melanie Holmes, Norman Howell, Mark Hughes, Justin Hynes, Rachel Ingham, Ellen Kolby, Bradley Lord, Bob McKenzie, Jon McAvoy, Jonny Noble, Jane Nottage, Ian Parkes, Ian Phillips, Nigel Roebuck, Holly Samos, Wolfgang Schattling, Eric Silbermann, Joe Saward, Jason Swales, David Tremayne and Byron Young.

And, finally, many thanks to David Luxton, Ian Chapman and everyone at Simon & Schuster for making this happen.

Maurice Hamilton
Cranleigh
January 2008